BEGINNING QUANTITATIVE RESEARCH

THE SAGE QUANTITATIVE RESEARCH KIT

Beginning Quantitative Research by *Malcolm Williams, Richard D. Wiggins, and the late W. Paul Vogt* is the first volume in *The SAGE Quantitative Research Kit*. This book can be used together with the other titles in the *Kit* as a comprehensive guide to the process of doing quantitative research, but it is equally valuable on its own as a practical introduction to completing quantitative research.

Editors of The SAGE Quantitative Research Kit:

Malcolm Williams – *Cardiff University, UK*

Richard D. Wiggins – *UCL Social Research Institute, UK*

D. Betsy McCoach – *University of Connecticut, USA*

Founding editor:

The late W. Paul Vogt – *Illinois State University, USA*

BEGINNING QUANTITATIVE RESEARCH

MALCOLM WILLIAMS
RICHARD D. WIGGINS
W. PAUL VOGT

Los Angeles | London | New Delhi
Singapore | Washington DC | Melbourne

THE SAGE QUANTITATIVE RESEARCH KIT

Los Angeles | London | New Delhi
Singapore | Washington DC | Melbourne

SAGE Publications Ltd
1 Oliver's Yard
55 City Road
London EC1Y 1SP

SAGE Publications Inc.
2455 Teller Road
Thousand Oaks, California 91320

SAGE Publications India Pvt Ltd
B 1/I 1 Mohan Cooperative Industrial Area
Mathura Road
New Delhi 110 044

SAGE Publications Asia-Pacific Pte Ltd
3 Church Street
#10-04 Samsung Hub
Singapore 049483

Editor: Jai Seaman
Assistant editor: Charlotte Bush
Production editor: Manmeet Kaur Tura
Copyeditor: QuADS Prepress Pvt Ltd
Proofreader: Elaine Leek
Indexer: Caroline Eley
Marketing manager: Susheel Gokarakonda
Cover design: Shaun Mercier
Typeset by: C&M Digitals (P) Ltd, Chennai, India
Printed in the UK

Library of Congress Control Number: 2020942572

British Library Cataloguing in Publication data

A catalogue record for this book is available from
the British Library

ISBN 978-1-5264-3214-8

At SAGE, we take sustainability seriously. Most of our products are printed in the UK using responsibly sourced
papers and boards. When we print overseas, we ensure sustainable papers are used as measured by the PREPS
grading system. We undertake an annual audit to monitor our sustainability.

DEDICATION

W. Paul Vogt†

With Richard D. Wiggins and Malcolm Williams, W. Paul Vogt was the founding editor of *The SAGE Quantitative Research Kit*. Paul sadly passed away, in 2016. However, before his death he contributed to this introductory volume. We had several discussions about what the finished volume should look like, and in completing it we have tried to remain as faithful as possible to Paul's methodological approach.

CONTENTS

LIST OF FIGURES, TABLES AND BOXES

List of figures

List of tables

List of boxes

ABOUT THE AUTHORS

Malcolm Williams is Professor and Co-director of the Cardiff Q-Step Centre for Quantitative Methods pedagogy. Until July 2014, he was the Director of the School of Social Sciences, at Cardiff, and prior to this he was Professor of Social Research Methodology at Plymouth University. He is the author/editor of 10 books and more than 100 articles/chapters. His primary research interest has been around methodological and philosophical issues in social research, particularly objectivity, probability, causality and representation. His most recent books are *Key Concepts in the Philosophy of Social Research* (2017) and *Realism and Complexity in Social Science* (2020). His past empirical research has included the measurement of homeless populations (using capture–recapture) and the analysis of longitudinal census data to explore household formation/dissolution and counter-urbanisation migration. In the last few years, his primary research interest has been in the pedagogy of quantitative methods.

Richard D. Wiggins is an Emeritus Professor in the Centre for Longitudinal Studies which is part of the newly formed UCL–Social Research Institute. He joined the Institute of Education, University of London, as Chair of Quantitative Social Science in 2007 and Head of the Department of Quantitative Social Science. From 2011 until 2013, he was Director of Methodology in the Centre for Longitudinal Studies, thereafter returning to his work as a researcher, doctoral supervisor and teacher. Prior to joining the Institute, he ran a successful master's programme in Social Research Methods and Statistics at City University, London. His early career included working in local and central government, epidemiological psychiatry and community medicine. His methodological interests include the longitudinal analysis of secondary data, survey design, attitude measurement and sampling methodology. His substantive research covers the impact of secondary schooling on adult outcomes, political trust, ageing and well-being.

W. Paul Vogt† was Emeritus Professor of Research Methods and Evaluation at Illinois State University where he won both teaching and research awards. He specialized in methodological choice and program evaluation and was particularly interested in ways to integrate multiple methods. His other books include *Tolerance & Education: Learning to Live with Diversity and Difference* (1998), *Quantitative Research Methods for Professionals* (2007) and *Education Programs for Improving Intergroup Relations* (coedited with Walter Stephan, 2004). He was also editor of four 4-volume sets in the series, *Sage Benchmarks in Social Research Methods: Selecting Research Methods* (2008), *Data Collection* (2010), *Quantitative Research Methods* (2011) and, with Burke Johnson, *Correlation and Regression Analysis* (2012). His most recent publications include the co-authored *When to Use What Research Design* (2012) and *Selecting the Right Analyses for Your Data: Quantitative, Qualitative, and Mixed Methods Approaches* (2014).

1

A GENERAL INTRODUCTION TO THIS KIT

MALCOLM WILLIAMS, RICHARD D. WIGGINS AND W. PAUL VOGT†

Chapter Overview

What is social research?

Social research is investigation in social science. Investigation allows social scientists to understand, explain and predict the social world. It is an enormously varied enterprise in both scale and methods. It encompasses everything from the micro-methods of small-group research, or research of individuals, to big data research, that gathers information from, sometimes, millions of social interactions. Unsurprisingly, the scale and variation in the nature of research leads to quite different methodological approaches. Broadly speaking, these can be divided into qualitative and quantitative methods, and whilst each of these has their origins in quite different philosophical traditions, in practice the divide is not always sharp. Indeed, many research programmes will employ both quantitative and qualitative approaches, in what is known as 'mixed methods' (Tashakkori & Teddle, 2010). Furthermore, some new approaches, in particular those that use data from new social media, blur the distinction between quantitative and qualitative research (Williams, 2021).

Social research matters because it is able to tell us what human societies are like. It is able to provide explanations of behaviour, beliefs and intentions at both micro and macro levels. Advanced societies cannot do without social research, and if there was ever any doubt in that, the COVID-19 pandemic, that began in early 2020, demonstrates this. Understanding the prevalence and spread of the disease, and the behaviours that accelerate or help to control these things, is as much about knowledge of the social phenomenon as it is about biology. For example, at a macro level what is the nature of population movement and behaviours that impact on prevalence and spread, and at a micro level how do we understand individual beliefs and behaviours?

This is but one example, current at the time of writing, but it takes little imagination to grasp the relevance of research to society in so many fields of, for example, criminal justice, education, housing, employment, gender and ethnicity. Many of these interact in complex ways, and so often social researchers must investigate problems that span these fields with a range of methodological tools. The tools, like the problems, range from the simple to the sophisticated, but behind these tools, there is methodological reasoning for their optimum use.

The SAGE 'Kits' (previously known as the *SAGE Qualitative Methods Kit*) and the current *SAGE Quantitative Research Kit*, aim to introduce social researchers to the tools and the reasoning behind their use.

What is quantitative research?

Quantitative research is about quantities. It is about measurement: how much of something there is, how long something has been happening or about explaining why something happened and possibly predicting if, or to what extent, it will happen in the future. Quantitative research is almost inevitably defined in contrast with qualitative research. And, of course, the converse is also true. Following that convention, the simplest, rule-of-thumb definition of quantitative research would be investigations in which the data that are collected and coded are expressible as numbers. By contrast, studies in which data are collected and coded as words would be instances of qualitative research. Weightier distinctions have also been important in discussions of research methods – distinctions bordering on epistemologies, worldviews and ontologies, to name a few. For our purposes, we will mostly leave those discussions to more philosophically directed books (Blaikie, 2007; Kincaid, 1996).

Quantitative research is grounded in the scientific tradition, so description and inference with the potential to lead to causal explanation and prediction are its core business. Its methods are those of the experiment, the social survey or the analysis of official statistics or naturally occurring data. It can take many forms from a local neighbourhood survey to large-scale population surveys with several thousand people taking part. It may be a carefully controlled experiment in a laboratory, or it might be 'big-data' analysis of millions of Twitter feeds (e.g. see Sloan, 2017). Increasingly, social researchers are conducting analyses using very large government-sponsored data sets, such as Understanding Society (www.understandingsociety. ac.uk/) or the Labour Force Survey (www.ons.gov.uk/surveys/informationforhouse holdsandindividuals/householdandindividualsurveys/labourforcesurveylfs) in the UK, and the Panel Study of Income Dynamics in the USA (https://psidonline.isr. umich.edu/). The number of participants in these studies run to many thousands, allowing quite sophisticated data analysis techniques to be used.

What *The SAGE Quantitative Research Kit* will do

The SAGE Quantitative Research Kit is intended to help and advise you through the design and execution of your research and, importantly, in analysing your results. Your research may consist of a relatively simple survey that you have to design from the beginning, or it may be a secondary analysis of existing data. In this Kit, you will be taken on a journey from initial methodological and design issues, through relatively basic statistical techniques, through sampling, experimental and survey design to analysis. Each volume is written by experts in the particular area of design or analysis. The volumes themselves are free-standing, but equally will help to build your knowledge base of quantitative methods from the basic, but important, techniques to quite advanced approaches to analysis.

At every stage the particular volume is a conduit to the literature in that approach and to research which has used this. Most of the volumes on analysis techniques are supported by online materials, though they are not necessarily detailed manuals on how to carry out a particular task in a menu-driven software package like IBM SPSS Statistics Software ("SPSS") (Pallant, 2020) or guides to writing your own programs in R (Wickham & Grolemund, 2017); they will tell where you can find such instructions.

About this volume

This volume is the starting point, or the foundation for the rest, and is aimed at those beginning quantitative research, or as a refresher in quantitative research before starting on the more specific volumes. The first part of this volume introduces you to some foundational theoretical and procedural concepts. Much of this is not covered elsewhere in *The SAGE Quantitative Research Kit*, though in line with other volumes, we will indicate where you can read in more depth on these topics. However, some of the chapters do introduce the subject matter of other volumes and might be seen as a 'primer' for these. So you will encounter some topics in this volume that you will encounter in much greater detail in later volumes. If you are new to social research, or to quantitative social research, the present volume will get you to the point of readiness to begin on the topic-specific volumes which follow.

In the next chapter, we begin with the starting point for any quantitative study – that of the research question. Where do **research questions** come from, how do we formulate them and how do we turn them into testable propositions that might be used either in surveys or experiments you design or in using existing data to answer your research question (or questions).

Chapter 3 is concerned with literature reviews and meta-analysis. A **literature review** is not an aesthetic critique but rather an overview and description of what we know of the topic area, whereas a meta-analysis, or systematic review, is a way to systematically conduct quantitative reviews of previous research.

In Chapter 4, we begin by considering the issue of research resources and the limits this places on research. However, most of the chapter introduces the four basic designs of social research: (1) experimental, (2) cross-sectional, (3) longitudinal and (4) case study and how these might be combined and how they relate to methods.

Research questions are closely linked to the population to which they apply. A 'population' may be people, or it could be schools, countries, companies and so on. In Chapter 5, we show how populations may be defined and how they may be sampled, in order to produce statistical inferences about them.

The research question, the type of population of interest and the way we access and sample it will make difference to the methods we use. We may, for example, choose to conduct a survey, which may be, for example, online, face to face or telephone.

Or, we may find that there are already secondary data available for the population, which requires us only to further analyse them. In Chapters 6 and 7, we describe some of these choices and crucially how they shape and will be shaped by our strategy for the analysis of the data.

In Chapter 8, we consider some of the background assumptions that shape our research and how we should act as ethical researchers. No research exists in a social vacuum, and the questions that interest us (or indeed that we are paid to research) are located in the social and political worlds we live in. So, given this, how can we be objective scientists who are also sensitive to the sensitivities, confidence and anonymity of our respondents?

The final chapter in this volume is the springboard into the others. In this chapter, we show how the concepts discussed in the book so far are carried forward by each of the other volumes and what you might expect in those volumes.

Chapter Summary

- This chapter introduces you to social research and why social research is relevant and important.
- The chapter describes quantitative and qualitative methods and their origins in different philosophical positions.
- The chapter is concerned with quantitative research as grounded in the scientific tradition of description, explanation and prediction.
- The chapter informs us what to expect from *The SAGE Quantitative Research Kit* and from this volume.

Further Reading

Blaikie, N. (2007). *Approaches to social enquiry* (2nd ed.). Polity.

This book is an excellent review of the ways in which social research can be carried out and the epistemologies that underpin them and sometimes create tensions between them.

Vogt, W. P. (2005). *Dictionary of statistics and methodology: A non-technical guide for the social sciences* (3rd ed.) Sage.

This dictionary is the 'go-to' place to clarify, in very basic terms, concepts and statistical language.

Williams, M. (2016). *Key concepts in the philosophy of social research*. Sage.

This book introduces the key philosophical issues (e.g. objectivity, probability and statistical reasoning) that underpin social research. Two other basic, but very accessible 'go-to' books for research terms, problems and concepts are the following:

Payne, G., & Payne, J. (2004). *Key concepts in social research*. Sage.

Salkind, N. (2012). *100 questions (and answers) about research methods*. Sage.

2

STARTING WITH THE BASICS: FROM RESEARCH PROBLEM TO VARIABLES

Chapter Overview

Research problems

The philosopher of science Karl Popper often said that we are students of a problem, not a discipline. All interesting and useful science begins with a problem to be solved. In social research, this is often a 'social problem', for example, why do young women not enter engineering professions in some countries but not others (Godfroy Genin & Pinault, 2011)? Does teenage drug taking lead to later relationship problems (Newcomb & Bentler, 1988)? How many homeless people are there in a particular city (Williams & Cheal, 2001)? Sometimes the problem may be more methodological, for example, can new social media methods better predict crime levels than traditional surveys (Williams et al., 2016), or it may 'test' some existing **theory**, such as migrants have greater resources in their originating society than non-migrants (Musgrove, 1963). An interesting characteristic of social research is what is a problem in one time or place may not be a problem in another time or place. So often research is comparative to test whether a 'problem' is location or time-specific. For example, see Zmerli and Hooghe (2011).

Not all problems can be successfully tackled through social research, either because (as in all science) we simply don't have the methodological capability or they are not problems that can be resolved with the resources available. Research questions often arise out of perceived social issues or problems that are considered of sufficient importance to a particular society to be the focus of social research, and consequently, it is these which often attract funding (more of this later), so what is a 'problem' (Bulmer, 2015)? Rarely are topics of interest completely novel; they usually have a history and quite frequently research has already been conducted and a body of knowledge exists in the research literature (we will say more about this below).

How do you identify a research problem? For many researchers, you just don't have to, because you have been hired to work within a research team as a researcher or doctoral candidate and are therefore investigating an identified research problem, but if you are a novice social researcher, needing to come up with your own ideas, there are a few things to consider.

Often, the problem will start off as something which interests you. So has it interested others? Has there been other research, either directly in the problem area or in a related one? How might this differ from what you want to research, either in terms of the population of interest, the sample or the methods used? Could you, at least partially, replicate a previous study? Sometimes your problem might be too 'broad', and you may wish to pick one specific and 'researchable' aspect of it. For example, each year one of us regularly supervises two or three undergraduate/masters research dissertations on the problem of 'homelessness'. You can't just research the 'problem of homelessness', but rather a very specific part of the problem needs to be identified.

What have been the 'routes' into homelessness in a particular city (and how might that differ from other locations)? What form does being homeless take, in a particular location? What are public attitudes toward rough sleepers? And so on.

Research questions

Research problems need to be expressed in the form of research questions that can be 'operationalised' into **hypotheses**, then measurements. A research question is simply a statement of what we want to know. It should be expressed fairly briefly, no more than a sentence or two. It may be quite a specific question that directly represents the research problem, such as why are there fewer women in senior academic roles than men. It may be a very localised and small-scale study, or one which aims to make generalisations across countries, comparisons between countries or through time. Some research problems, particularly those that are explored in larger studies, may have more than one research question, in order to explore a quite broad area of concern or interest. The above problem, concerning women entering engineering, is a problem for certain countries, but it leads to many specific research questions, such as: Are educational experiences that 'gender' engineering present in countries that have larger numbers of women entering the profession? Do universities have positive action programmes? Are subjects 'gendered' in schools?

Some research questions just cannot be answered, or answered in the context of their being posed. For example,

> *Do young people feel less optimistic about their future?* This is far too vague. In principle, something like it could be answered, but defining *optimism*, and *future*, would be necessary – and indeed what counts as a young person. Moreover, to be able to say anything, there would need to be a comparison with the attitudes of previous cohorts of young people (or indeed people in other age groups).

> *Should people become vegan?* The problem here is it begins with a value statement, which implies either pro- or anti-veganism. But attitudes toward a vegan diet/lifestyle, amongst vegans and non-vegans, could be researched.

> *Does exposure to violent media images lead to violent behaviour?* There are all sorts of problems here. What counts as a violent image? What counts as violent behaviour? But mostly isolating the media images from other stimulants to violence is impossible. Actually, in a large enough study, with enough data, the effects of other stimulants might be controlled for, but this is a question beyond the resources and abilities of most new researchers.

> *Why do people commit suicide?* This is, in principle, unanswerable, because they are already dead! Analysis of suicide notes might provide some reasons, but the reasons might actually be latent. Unsuccessful suicides are often not intended to be successful, so this is not a group that can answer the question successfully.

The above examples show that some things just cannot be done, but the areas of interest may be amenable to research, if answerable questions can be posed.

Whilst the initial framing of the question or questions may be broad-brush, soon it is necessary to turn them into research hypotheses and then measures, 'operationalised' within a survey or experiment – in other words, turned into measurements that can empirically answer the question. The population of interest must also be defined. So, for example, an exploration of student views on research methods teaching would lead us to ask which subject, or subjects, are the students studying? Are they undergraduate or postgraduate, in one university in one country or a range of universities in one, or more, countries? The simple rule is that a sharp question will provide a sharp answer. The opposite, of course, is true!

The role of theory in research

Quite often, the research question is grounded in a theory, which you are testing, either in an amended form or in a new context. All research implies theoretical assumptions, but good research sets out by making those assumptions clear. So what is a theory?

A 'theory' is a proposition, or set of propositions, about relationships between phenomena. It proposes that something is, or isn't the case. In particular, if a theory is true, it implies how the world must be, or acts in certain ways. A theory should have testable consequences. In other words, it should predict or forbid certain things to happen and should be able to derive measurements from those predictions that will allow us to say whether or not something is the case, or how much or how many of something. Finally, the scope of a theory can vary, and this should be written into it to begin with. Some theories might be very localised, and others have a much broader scope. An example of the former might be that a particular local public transport initiative will reduce traffic congestion. In this case, local factors will play an important role, but nevertheless in formulating such a localised 'theory', one should draw on data from other locations. It might well turn out that one's localised theory is not local at all. An example of more ambitious theory testing might be in the exploration of the social composition of recent migrant refugees from troubled Middle Eastern countries, in order to assess their potential for economic and social integration. You may theorise that the majority of them come from an educated or merchant class in their home country, and if you did you would be testing the theory of migratory elites, proposed by Frank Musgrove, in the 1960s, which broadly states that migrants in a developed, or relatively developed, society will be those who have comparatively greater resources to permit migration (Musgrove, 1963). Now, it may be that you are able to confirm that this was indeed the case, or if you discover that the migrants were not from such classes, the theory would be falsified – at least in this instance, and you would need to show why this was the case and possibly amend the theory to take new localised circumstances into consideration.

Theory comes in different forms. You will see many publications under the heading 'social theory'. Much, though not all, of this constitutes 'grand societal theories' grounded in philosophical assumptions that have a broad explanatory reach, for example, Giddens (1993) 'structuration theory', or Bauman's (1999) 'liquid modernity'. Indeed, whilst these theories may be intuitively plausible, it is very difficult to derive propositions from them that may be empirically tested in order to show whether, or to what extent, they are correct. Some theories with a wide societal or historic reach are indeed testable, but these are usually expressed in clear terms, which define their scope and limits. Indeed, the migratory elites theory, mentioned above, is one such example.

Then, at the opposite end of the scale comes what we might term *experiential theory*, because it is suggested by our direct experiences of the world. Such 'theories' are often hunches based on what we see, hear or people tell us. For example, one of us believes that the readers of certain right-wing UK newspapers are more selfish in their everyday manners, and this belief arises from observations of such people's behaviour on train journeys. Now, this may or may not be true, but whether it is, or not, there is not a scrap of prior theory that has informed this hunch, and in order to turn it into good scientific research, one would first need to find evidence of such prior theory and possibly actual empirical studies. Finally, having done this, it would need to be tested through the derivation of empirical measures. But a great deal of research, rightly or wrongly, does begin from such hunches, or politicians' ideas or fads. The former British prime minister David Cameron set at least two such hares running in 2010/2011, with his vague concept of the 'Big Society' and his wish to measure happiness![i]

Most theories that social researchers develop or test are 'theories of the middle range'. This concept was first suggested by the US sociologist Robert Merton (1968) and has since been developed as 'middle-range realism' by the British sociologist Ray Pawson (2000).

Middle-range theory consolidates propositional statements and observed regularities and shows how these might be tested empirically. As in the natural sciences, the 'scope' of the theory is stated – that is, what would count as a confirmation that the theory was right and what would count as a falsification, to show it to be wrong. For example, recent work in nursing research (Elo et al., 2013) is concerned with well-

---

[i]Many psychologists believe that happiness can be measured. See, for example, https://worlddata baseofhappiness.eur.nl/hap_quer/introtext_measures3.pdf.

being from the viewpoint of people themselves – in this case an elderly population in Scandinavia. Though the concept of well-being is commonplace, in this case it was not defined in advance: the definition was based on the experiences of the study subjects. It began with the hypothesis that the environment was considered as a source of well-being, with the elderly seen as fulfilling their needs and the environment as a resource that contributes to well-being. The research had four stages: (1) the creations of concepts were described inductively through concept synthesis, (2) relationships between the concepts were examined to set up a hypothetical model, (3) hypotheses were set up to verify the concepts and to test possible models and (4) the verification and presentation of the theory (Elo et al., 2013). Note that within this process two things are going on. Firstly, a theory is developed from a concept of well-being that was not predefined but hypothesised as originating in people themselves. This was then empirically tested and a new theory created, which itself was capable of being tested under other circumstances.

Variables

Once we have a clear research question, have reviewed the literature in order to ascertain what previous empirical or theoretical work has been done and have located our question in an appropriate theoretical framework, we must operationalise the research question or questions into research hypotheses and then into **variables** that can be measured. This is sometimes called 'descending the ladder of abstraction'.

Quantitative research is usually 'variable-based'. A *variable* is a feature or aspect of your topic that can take on different values – typically referred to as a characteristic of your unit of analysis (person, neighbourhood etc.). A variable tends to differ depending on its relationship to one or more other variables, for example, the level of unemployment by region.

Variables are usually classified as independent, sometimes called the predictor variable (the presumed cause in a relationship) or dependent (the assumed effect), sometimes called the outcome variable. So, for example, labour unrest in a region (dependent/outcome) could be related to a decline in employment in that region (independent/predictor), or the voter turnout for particular parties or factions in a region (dependent/outcome) could be related to the degree of voter dissatisfaction in that region (independent/predictor).

But the independent–dependent variable relationship is rarely a direct one, and other kinds of variables usually intervene. A *moderator* variable is one that shapes or influences the relation between an independent and a dependent variable. For example, we may be interested in the relationship between labour unrest (dependent) and a decline in employment (independent), but the relationship may be *moderated* or influenced by which part of the country your respondents reside. In this sense, region would be regarded as a moderator.

Moderator variables are typically distinguished from *mediating* variables. These are variables which 'transmit the effects of another variable'. For example, parents 'transmit' their social status to their children directly, but they may also do this by exercising choice over the kind of education their child receives (Goldthorpe, 2016).

Finally, there are confounding variables, whereby there are two independent variables, whose effects cannot be separated. For example, if a teacher X used textbook A in a class and teacher Y used textbook B and students were given tests of their learning achievement, the 'independent' variables (the textbooks and the teachers' teaching effectiveness) would be 'confounded', because there would be no way to tell whether any difference observed between the classes, in achievement (the dependent variable), was caused by either or both of the dependent variables.

To return to the labour unrest example, a theory may specify the relationship between the dependent, moderator and independent variables and will constitute the theory to be tested; that is, unemployment causes labour unrest, because it depresses wages, and each element of the theory is represented by a variable.

But it may not be that simple. It is unlikely, for example, that even in industries that have experienced wage decline there is not always labour unrest. Further variables will need to be added and tested in the 'model' (more on models in *The SAGE Quantitative Research Kit*, Volumes 8, 9 and 10). It may be that in some industries labour is not 'organised' in trade unions, or the enterprises may be very small, or employ more casual labour. We now consider variables as being ascribed to a case. **Cases** are typically individuals who are the subjects of our inquiry.

Cases

On the face of it, a 'case' is quite intuitive, it is usually an individual from whom we can obtain information. This information might be derived from official statistics, or other secondary sources, and comprise things like age, sex, occupation, address, record of severe illness (e.g. cancer) and so on. Alternatively, such information, alongside other attributes, behaviours, attitudes and beliefs, may have been collected via a survey. But all of this information will relate to a 'case' and be operationalisable into variables. But in order to conduct analyses between cases, we will need to have the same information for each case. So, in the simplest of examples, in order to ascertain any difference between males and females on a question of interest, we must have information of each 'case' about whether they are male or female. If we do not have this information, then this is called 'missing data'. Analyses can be conducted when some data are missing, but this requires particular procedures which make assumptions about the mechanism of 'missingness'. We discuss this further in Chapter 7.

Though the case is usually an individual person, it does not have to be. It may be a country, a company, a school or an historical event. Some researchers, nowadays, might draw their cases from more than one level and combine the analyses at each level, say an individual school pupil, a school and a locality. This is called multilevel analysis and is explained in Volume 9.

Whether one chooses individuals, schools, countries and so on as the 'case', in the analysis itself these are then described as the 'unit of analysis'.

Research hypotheses and measures

The term *hypothesis* has been mentioned above a few times. Logically, hypotheses and theories are equivalent, they are each propositional statements, but hypotheses are used in two ways in social research and science more generally. Firstly, and in the sense above, they are statements which make specific testable links between theories and measurement, and secondly, they are statistical propositional statements. A statistical hypothesis is initially posed negatively and is called the 'null hypothesis' (its opposite is usually called the 'alternative hypothesis'). If something is found to be statistically significant (i.e. the finding is not due to chance), then the researcher *rejects* the null hypothesis and *accepts* the alternative one. Statistical hypotheses may be derived from research hypotheses. Statistical hypotheses and hypothesis testing are described in detail in Volume 3.

Theories help us to generate fairly informal research questions, that will guide the research, but they need to be firmed up into research hypotheses that will propose what should happen, or is forbidden from happening. These hypotheses are tested and may confirm, partially confirm or falsify a theory (Stinchcombe, 1968).

Hypotheses are testing a theory, and to do this they must propose measures. Assuming that you can identify a causal effect, the hypotheses must propose independent variables that can explain that effect. There does not have to be one single independent variable, because as we noted above there may also be variables which moderate or mediate the relationship of an independent and a dependent variable. But what is important is that the research hypotheses clearly state what relations between these variables are expected. Some good practice in formulating research hypotheses might be something like this:

- Are you clear in the language you are using to formulate the hypothesis?
- Are you specifically representing the key elements of the theory in the hypotheses?
- Does the hypothesis include both an independent and a dependent variable? Have these been clearly identified?

- Are there moderating or mediating variables that must be taken into account? Could some variables be confounding?
- Does the hypothesis explain what you expect to happen during your research?
- Can the hypothesis be successfully tested through the methods proposed (e.g. a survey, a secondary analysis or an experiment)?

Here is a brief example from counterurbanisation research. Counterurbanisation is a 'middle-range' theory, which aims to explain why people move from urban (often cities) to rural or 'peri-urban' areas (Champion, 1994, 2001). One of us conducted research on counterurbanisation migration to Cornwall, UK. The original theory proposes that migrants will themselves become economically better off in their destination and that their destination will also benefit the community economically. Neither was the case in Cornwall, so the research aimed to find out why. Here are two of the research hypotheses and their measures. There were more hypotheses, and the one given below is a somewhat simplified account (Buck et al., 1993; Williams & Champion, 1998):

> *Hypothesis 1*: migrants move to Cornwall primarily for its environmental attraction, rather than economic advantage.
>
> Operationalised through independent variables, such as attitudes to environment, current economic resources, employment attitudes and intentions. Also, there were proposed moderators, such as age, education and social class.
>
> *Hypothesis 2:* migrants will have amassed sufficient economic assets to be able to move to Cornwall.
>
> Operationalised through independent variables, such as housing status and employment prior to migration. Moderating variables included region of origin, household composition and size.

Identifying cases, units of analysis, research hypotheses and variables is not the end of the matter, for there are further rungs on that ladder of abstraction! The variables must now be turned into measures in a survey or experiment. There is much more about this in Volumes 2, 3, 4, 6 and 8. But for the moment, it is worth noting that the measures that will operationalise your variables will have to be derived by you in a new survey (though you may use those that others have previously used), but increasingly researchers are turning to the secondary data sources. In this case, you have to try to find existing measures, that were used to obtain the data for the original survey, that will be appropriate for the variables you want to measure. Sometimes, a 'proxy' can stand in for what you want. For example, the UK censuses do not measure housing quality, but they do measure whether or not a dwelling has central heating. The absence of central heating is a reasonably good proxy for poor-quality housing. However, these censuses do not measure income at all, so to find out about individual socio-economic status a whole lot of variables together, such as social class, occupation, location, education and so on, must be used.

Description and explanation and causes

Description and explanation are the cornerstones of science, and all explanation begins with some kind of description. National censuses, official statistics and other large-scale surveys are descriptive in nature. That is, they take a number of phenomena that are considered useful to measure and measure them. This does not mean that the questions asked do not have a purpose, as we will explain in more detail in the final chapter; all research, however 'neutral' it may appear to be, is for a purpose and is socially located. Moreover, descriptive surveys may then be utilised by others to provide explanations. For example, UK Longitudinal Census data can be used to provide detailed descriptions of change over time, in things like housing, migration, change in socio-economic status or household change, but the data do not themselves provide explanation, something more is required – a theory which purports to explain such change, but can then be tested using the descriptive data. Some research examples can be found at www.indigo-sandbox.ucl.ac.uk/celsius/research/columns/research-projects.

Before a researcher can move to trying to explain something, she must be sure her data are adequately describing the phenomenon in question. This description has two dimensions. Firstly, the measures themselves must measure those things they purport to measure (more of this in Volumes 4 and 5). Secondly, if one is using sample data, then the sample must adequately describe the population – again this will be discussed in more detail in Volume 2.

So, description precedes explanation, and a study may only be descriptive. An explanation is the answer to a why, or how, question. Why is there less social mobility in country X as compared to country Y? How do women negotiate male working environments? Often explanations are answers to causal questions, but causal questions – though certainly answerable with quantitative data – are rarely straightforward. We will say more about this, in relation to choosing a research design, in Chapter 4, whilst a particular approach to causal analysis, in quantitative research, is the topic of Volume 10.

There is one last thing to say about explanation and description. Explanations are predictions, indeed logically they are isomorphic (Schlipp, 1991, p. 556) – that is, logically each implies the other. A prediction that labour unrest will follow from high levels of unemployment implies an explanation. But more strongly, a successful explanation that in context C^1 labour unrest did follow from high unemployment, but was moderated by wage reduction, provides a prediction to be tested in context C^2.

Causes

Explanation usually implies causes. In quantitative research, we answer causal questions either through experimental or survey methods. Now, experiments in the social world cannot be the same as those in the laboratory, say for chemists or physicists. Firstly, because the social world is more complex, and secondly, the laboratory is often too much of an artificial environment to produce results that can hold much beyond the laboratory setting, so social researchers must conduct their experiments in the field – that is, in the natural social setting. But never mind, the logic is the same. The population is divided into two samples, the first is the experimental group, in which there is some kind of 'treatment', say an educational or health intervention with this group, and the second is the 'control' group, with whom there is no intervention. If other environmental effects can be accounted for, then a change in the experimental group is said to be caused by the intervention. But there is much more to it than that, and the logic and practice of experiments is the topic of Volume 6. Indeed, in many circumstances even experiments in the field are not possible and causal explanation must be sought through analysis of survey data.

But be forewarned that there is no concept in these volumes more troublesome than causality. As the philosopher Nancy Cartwright remarked, 'One word, many things' (Cartwright, 2004). There is disagreement amongst both researchers and philosophers about what a cause is. One common formulation goes like this:

> To attribute cause, for X to cause Y, three conditions are necessary (but not sufficient): (1) X must precede Y, (2) X and Y must covary (i.e. associated together) and (3) no rival explanations account as well for the covariance of X and Y.

Causal relations may be simple or multiple. In simple causation, whenever the first event (the cause – represented by the independent variable) happens, the second effect always follows (represented by the dependent variable). However, simple causation is all but absent in the social world, and multiple causation is all but universal. Multiple causes may be such that any one of several causes can produce the same effect. Homelessness, for example, may be 'caused' by many different antecedent conditions, and homelessness itself causes other things, for example, ill health. Furthermore, the same conditions in one time or place context may cause different things.

An important divide in thinking, in quantitative methods, is the extent to which causal inference can be derived only from multiple probabilistic associations in models or the extent to which causes can be 'interpreted' from models (Byrne, 2002; Freedman, 2011; Williams, 2021). These two approaches can be found in the other volumes in this *SAGE Quantitative Research Kit*. In Volume 6, the emphasis, following Campbell and Stanley (1963), derives from the logic of the experiment. Did the treatments within the experiment make a difference (internal validity), and to what extent is a causal effect generalisable to other populations, contexts or settings (external validity)? In Volume 10, a quite different approach is taken where the simple cause–effect model is superseded by a complexity approach which sees outcomes nested in a vast array of antecedent conditions, in which a simple causal model would under-describe complex and emergent social processes and mechanisms.

Amongst the authors of this volume, one of us (Paul) takes a position, rather closer to the first approach, and the other two of us (Dick and Malcolm) take something of an intermediate position, which sees causes as complex, but also amenable to statistical analysis.

But let us try to simplify for the moment. Causal explanations are grounded in the variable analysis we described above. When developing causal explanations from survey data, one must move beyond the association of two variables, though they often start there. Indeed, it is often said that statistical correlation is not causation (though as Matthew McBee notes in Volume 10, it is always the case that causation implies correlation).

Two variables are often statistically associated – that is, their occurrence together is seen to be more than chance. For example, a society with large numbers of homeless people may be one with high unemployment, but there again it may not. This raises all sorts of interesting questions. Why, for example, is it that there is an association in one place (*A*) between homelessness and unemployment but not in another (*B*) (Bramley & Fitzpatrick, 2018)?

What is the direction of causality in *A*? Does unemployment cause homelessness, or is it the other way around? Or (and in fact this is closer to the truth) the cause operates in both directions over time?

But in place *B*, there is relatively little homelessness, despite high unemployment. Finally, there is somewhere called *C* where there is low unemployment but high levels of homelessness.

Now, let us assume your measurement of homelessness and unemployment is the same in *A*, *B* and *C*; then the explanation (which will be different in each case) will require the addition of new variables in an explanatory model.

Notice, we have used the word *model* here to indicate a statistical model, usually with three or (a lot) more variables. In linear models, causal explanation is derived from the best 'fitting' statistical model. At this stage, that may sound mysterious, but in Volumes 9 and 10 much will be revealed in the matter of causal explanation and the kinds of models we use to achieve it!

One last note of caution when one searches for causes in quantitative data. It is the dog that did not bark! By this we mean that causal attribution must ultimately rest on that which is measured. If it is not measured, it cannot contribute to the 'cause' in the model. And it is often the case that something important was not measured! This is referred to in the literature as 'omitted variable bias' (Riegg, 2008). There are also models (structural equation models) which aim to take account of variables that cannot be measured directly by defining 'unobserved' or 'latent variables'. These are introduced in Volume 9. We will return to causes in Chapter 4.

Conclusion

In this chapter, we have briefly outlined some of the methodological issues that a researcher must consider at the beginning of the research process. There are commonalities across all research: that you must begin with a research question and that inevitably you are testing some kind of theory, whether it is local, informal or experiential, or a much more formal and established theory. You must descend the 'ladder of abstraction' from the broad brush of your initial question or questions down to specific measures – or the adoption of existing measures in secondary sources.

Finally, all experienced researchers know that any research project is linked to the resources that are available. These may be access to a particular population in order to derive a sample (this is discussed primarily in Volume 4 but also in Volume 5) or to have the time and the person power to collect and analyse the data.

Chapter Summary

- This chapter is an introduction to some of the foundational concepts in quantitative research. It begins with the idea that all research is problem solving, but these problems have to be turned into research questions that can be answered. Research questions are formulated in the context of theory – What is a theory and what kinds of theories are there?
- The chapter then goes on to describe what is meant by a 'variable' and how these relate to 'cases'. Having formulated a research question(s), this needs to be operationalised through identified variables into research hypotheses.
- Finally, the chapter discusses the role of research in description and explanation and also how quantitative research is able to identify causes and the limits to this.

Further Reading

This chapter is about the journey from theory to planning your research. There are many excellent books in this area. Here, we suggest three of the clearest guides to this process.

Frankfort-Nachmias, C., & Nachmias, D. (1996). *Research methods in the social sciences*. Arnold.

Now something of a classic, this book is a general introduction to research methods, but because of this it describes the journey from theory to carrying out research within that broader context.

Litwin, M. (1995). *How to measure survey reliability and validity*. Sage.

This is a short book; nevertheless, it provides a very clear non-technical understanding of reliability and different types of validity and how they may be achieved.

Byrne, D. (2002). *Interpreting quantitative data*. Sage.

This book takes a realist approach to quantitative research and emphasises the importance of causality as complex and takes a sophisticated approach to measurement.

3

LITERATURE REVIEWS AND META-ANALYSES

Chapter Overview

Introduction

Once a research question or problem has been identified, the next logical step is to begin finding what prior research has been done on the topic. There is something of a paradox in this step because one of the most effective ways to seek gaps in knowledge, focus your research question or refine your problem is to conduct a good review of the literature on the topic. A good review leads to a good problem statement, but a good problem statement helps you focus the review. This is less of a paradox than it might seem, however. Rather, reviewing the research literature and refining the research question are complementary, iterative, activities. Often, literature reviews are not finalised until nearly the end of the research.

The remainder of the activities discussed in this volume – from research design, to sampling plan, to methods of data collection, to the ethical conduct of research and to devising analysis plans – can all be enhanced by effective reviewing of the research literature.

Effective researchers in quantitative social research have nearly always based their work on the efforts of those who have investigated the same or similar topics. What is new in recent years is the increased rigour with which reviews of the research literature have been conducted. Much more effort is paid now than it once was to conducting reviews in ways that are transparent, systematic and rigorous (Gough et al., 2012). The idea, often repeated, is to treat the data of a literature review with the same seriousness as any other data.

These tendencies in research reviewing were greatly stimulated by the emergence in the 1970s of Cochrane reviews in biomedical research and meta-analysis in psychology and education (see https://uk.cochrane.org and Higgins & Thomas, 2019). A meta-analysis proceeds by combining the information (evidence) across a number of systematic reviews. Both were stimulated by the enormous expansion of research in these and related areas and the proliferation of findings that were increasingly hard to summarise using merely verbal methods.

Conducting literature reviews

The kind of literature review undertaken will itself depend on the kind of research that is to be conducted. A researcher in a local council whose brief it is to find out citizens' views on public transport provision would search for studies in other communities, possibly looking at the ways in which the public were consulted. The search would not usually take the researcher into the academic literature of transport and infrastructure etc. However, an academic researcher who wanted to examine the social relations of transport provision – say a new high-speed railway line – might examine a wider academic literature on environmental effects, the political economy of local capital and the social relations of spatial communities.

As a rough rule, the more academic or theoretically ambitious the study, the deeper and wider the literature review. Academic research usually requires a thorough search of electronic databases, typically Google Scholar or Web of Science. Though this is nowadays unavoidable, it does not exhaust the search possibilities; moreover some experience and skill is often required to find the literature in a particular area.

Certainly, in academia, there is a pressure to become increasingly systematic in reviews of the research literature, and this has been exacerbated by the problem of how to address and handle the growing number of publications in most areas of research. This has been made more complex as a result of the rapid spread of open-source publications; these have proliferated and differ greatly in their standards. Open-source publications can offer free access to readers because authors rather than readers or sub-scribers pay the cost of making access freely available. But beware! Quite a few of these are little more than fraudulent schemes for collecting publication fees from vulnerable authors (see the exposé in Bohannon, 2013). The author sent a bogus article, with obvi-ous methodological flaws, to hundreds of journals, and the great majority accepted it for publication – after the payment of a fee. And, as if fraudulent journals were not enough, some authors have found ways to corrupt the peer review process at legitimate, highly respected, journal publishers, such as Springer and Sage (Haug, 2015). Fortunately for social researchers, the pressures leading to such corruption are dramatically less intense in social than in natural and biomedical research, so the problems, while not absent in the social sciences, are of less concern for most readers of this book.

Conducting a literature review, where the breadth and depth of research studies that a reviewer of the research literature must cover, is huge and dramatically big-ger than it once was. This presents an important challenge for you to tackle. Firstly, you need a set of tools to do the job, which is more than just search a term or two. Though it is possible to at least begin informally, firstly, do not be too literal: enter-ing the search terms 'crime and poverty' will produce some 'hits', but a bit of lateral thinking might be required, say by thinking of what kind of poverty might be associ-ated with particular kinds of criminality? Once some key literature has been identi-fied, it is then possible to follow up other material through looking at their lists of references. Eventually, the same papers will start to make a number of appearances, and one gets some sense that the key literature has been identified. Although not necessarily a mark of quality, some papers will be cited more than others. For exam-ple, Mike Savage and Roger Burrows (2007) published a paper titled 'The Coming Crisis of Empirical Sociology'. In their own words, this paper was something of a polemic and not the most considered or important paper in this debate, but it was seminal, and by mid-2018, it was cited in more than 800 other publications, so if you were researching this topic, the paper would be unavoidable.

Moving beyond simply putting search terms into Google Scholar, there is a familiar and well-developed set of tools for conducting literature reviews and a set of standards and practices that can help you along your way. Firstly, you will need to explain exactly where and how you searched for studies to include in your review in any background introduction to your own research (in, say, an academic paper or research report). You should begin with your research question/problem and the variables you identified to study it. This can be a bit trickier than it might at first seem because the same or similar variables might go by different names in the work of researchers in different disciplines. Hence, the issue with rather vague terms such as *crime* and *poverty*. So if you were studying the set of variables reaching from unemployment to declining wages, to labour unrest, you might find several different ways to measure or characterise these variables. Thus, you will need to get familiar with the literature in order to search it for relevant studies, so it is OK to begin informally as suggested above.

Though there are no algorithms for how to proceed with a literature review, there are useful guidelines, especially for *finding* potential studies to include in your review, but there can be no invariant rules, because, in the last analysis, interpreting and integrating the findings of prior work in an area is a matter of interpretation and understanding.

Electronic databases are indispensable in your searching, in part because they often provide lists of synonyms. There are about 10 such bibliographic databases that social researchers use. It is rare to see a research review that uses them all and even rarer to see a serious review that uses only one. You need to use more than one because, depending on your topic, each has its own strengths and weaknesses, and there will be a large commonality of the literature in each. Typically, a reviewer uses three to five databases. The obvious place to start is Google Scholar because it is easy to access and use, but more sophisticated ones include Social Science Citation Index, Sociofile, psycINFO, Sociological Abstracts and Web of Science. We don't specify what index to use for what purposes or exactly how to use each because they all come with intuitively obvious instructions. But here are a few tips.

Start by looking for previous reviews of the literature on your topic. Then, focus first on the most recent studies because these often capture what was learned in earlier studies. Examining what was learned in earlier studies is often called the *ancestry method*. You study the ancestors or progenitors of important recent studies in your field (and this may be where the citations and lists of references in a paper will help). Then, for a next step, you can use the Social Science Citation Index or Google Scholar to enquire into the uses others made of these ancestors, which is sometimes called the *descendant method*.

As you do more and more of this early reviewing, your familiarity with the topic and how it is studied in the research literature will grow, as will your ability to search effectively. This will lead to a summary of your search procedures. Most reviews now begin with a formal statement, such as the following hypothetical example, which is shorter than typical.

One of us (Paul) initially searched for the key terms *unemployment, wages* and *labour unrest*, using the databases above. He used studies only in English published since 1960, studying nations that were at the time members of the OECD (Organisation for Economic Co-operation and Development). He found 200 studies that met the initial selection criteria. Of these, all but 89 were eliminated because of various technical problems, including lack of adequate information on the key variables. It was very important to include detailed exclusion and inclusion criteria. For example, some studies may contain duplicate data; other primary studies could contain separate data in the same work, as in one focusing on two strikes or another focusing on a boycott and another strike.

The technicalities of the search

Here are a few points of a more technical nature about searching strategies:

- 'Boolean' statements or 'operators' (named after the logician George Boole) are absolutely essential when using electronic databases. The three key ones are (1) AND, (2) OR and (3) NOT. They help you specify the ways in which you want to link and define your variables. For example, if you want to look into the full example model – unemployment → wages → labour unrest – you would want to link the three components by ANDs. OR can dramatically increase the number of 'hits' in a search. Finally, if you wanted to include certain types of labour unrest, such as strikes and boycotts, you might say strikes OR boycotts; this would link the two. Conversely, if you were interested in strikes, but not boycotts, you could sever the two with NOT.
- Finally, you can broaden the search by using so-called wildcards. These are symbols (the symbols differ from one database to another) that allow you to include other versions of a word. One common symbol is the asterisk; for example, tolera* would get you *tolerance, tolerate* and *toleration*.
- It is also useful to look for antonyms, terms with the opposite meaning. In the case of a study of tolerance (conducted by Paul), the most important antonym was discrimination; prejudice was a close second. Using a wildcard entry, discrimina*, yielded studies with the key terms *discrimination, discriminatory, discriminate* and *discriminating*, or one could have entered an opposite, such as inclus*.
- The initial searching will usually turn up dozens, perhaps hundreds, of primary studies that you could consider including in your review. Given the tendency for the size of a literature review on a topic to get away from you, it is crucial to keep a record of your work as you go along, noting where and how you have searched and what you have found. This should include studies that are clearly important to your study.
- Almost as important as well are probably those studies that you exclude, that at first might have seemed promising but turned out not to be so. Keeping track

of searches and the initial results saves huge amounts of time. Many researchers find spreadsheets the easiest way to do this essential sorting, indexing and record keeping. One way to supplement your spreadsheet is with fieldnotes (perhaps in the form of a journal) to help you recall how and why you made the many decisions that make up the typical research review.

- One of the features of a pool of studies you are likely to notice is biases in the studies you found. Writers on the subject of literature reviewing have most often focused on *publication bias*, which is a tendency to ignore research that has not been published and which, in turn, is often held to stem from too much reliance on studies which report 'statistically significant' findings (typically, summary statistics with low *p*-values). More important perhaps, especially in the realm of social research, are biases stemming from under-represented groups in the authorship of research studies or biases resulting from inadequate attention to gender, ethnic and/or religious minorities. No matter how perfect your summary of the existing research, it can itself be no better than the research being summarised.

Quality control in literature reviews

The above should help you to find the literature, but having found it, how do you critically assess it? Implied, in the above, is the caution that not all literature is equal! Therefore, you need to assess the nature and quality of the literature you have found. Search engines will often list the most cited papers/book and so on, first. But this can be something of a beauty competition. As we noted, the Savage and Burrows (2007) paper was intended to stimulate debate, which it did, but as the debate went on, several later papers were much more evidence focused than this. But in any search, the Savage and Burrows paper will be the most cited (indeed, we have just added to this!).

There are a few things to bear in mind, when assessing the literature.

What are the methods, research and sampling strategies? The literature will often cite both qualitative and quantitative sources. Now, the former may be valuable and insightful studies, but equally they may be early exploratory studies, or ones that investigate a specific aspect of the problem. Also, there are limits to how much one can generalise from qualitative research (Williams, 2000). Now, assuming (say) the paper you are assessing is based on quantitative research, was this primary or secondary data? Both are fine, but both have their limitations. In the first case, how big was the sample and what was the sampling method? We would always favour a probability sample over a non-probability sample (see Chapter 5 and Volume 4). What was the mode of data collection? Face to face, telephone, online and so on? What was the response rate and the item non-response for particular questions? Some of the same questions arise in secondary analysis, but there are others too – for example, were proxy variables used, because direct measures could not be obtained? (See Volume 5.)

Were the findings controversial? Search engines, such as Google Scholar, will have links to the citations for a paper/book. In these, you might find theoretical or methodological questions raised about the original publication. Indeed, there may be a debate. In this *SAGE Quantitative Research Kit*, you will hear a lot about 'statistical significance' and a fair bit about 'significance testing', so try entering the simple terms *significance testing* into Google Scholar, and you will unearth an important and lively debate!

Although the publications you find may be within the same area of interest, they may begin from quite different theoretical positions. It follows from this: that what is investigated, how it is investigated and the conclusions drawn may be quite different from each other.

What is the 'quality' of the publication? By this, we mean what were the quality controls to ensure the rigour of what was published? There is a rough hierarchy here. At the top come peer-reviewed journal articles, and at the head of these come those with the highest citation index scores. It does not automatically follow that a paper in a journal with a high citation score[i] is 'better' than one in a journal with a low citation score, but the high-scoring journal will almost certainly have more exacting standards for publication acceptance (and consequently reject weaker papers). Next, come books. Again, not all books are the same! Some are 'monographs', which have usually been through some form of peer review and are (anyway) often the work of established scholars. A tip here is to look for the reviews of these monographs. Then, there are textbooks, which rarely use primary data and are not intended to be platforms for research. Finally, there are reports. Some of these, coming from funded research projects in universities, are often very rigorous and may well provide more methodological detail than journal articles. Some may well have online links to the data sets and research in the project.

Primary and secondary sources

This is not the same as primary and secondary data, but rather the first is directly reporting on research, and the second is citing other people's work. The second you should be careful of. There is no epistemological or methodological equivalence between (say) a publication that reports directly on findings from a study and one in which the author is simply stating his or her view on a topic. For example, a paper may just speculate that the increase in 'living alone' is due to new forms of intimacy (Bawin-Legros, 2004), whereas another paper may report on a large sample study

---

[i]See www.scimagojr.com/journalrank.php?area=3300 for a list of citation scores of social science journals and an explanation of citation scoring.

which described patterns of living alone and is therefore based on empirical evidence (Ware et al., 2007). One may indeed mention the first, but more attention should be given to the second.

In the publications, discovered commonalities and differences in approaches and findings will emerge. Here, synthesis is needed (e.g. Stahl & Miller, 1989). A good strategy is to list the approaches and findings in a table and look for similarity and difference. If, say, three studies, using a similar methodological strategy, produced similar results, this is interesting, but equally so if one produced a different result, this is even more interesting.

In most literature reviews, a plethora of publications will be discovered. Some will be absolutely central to your own research, others peripheral, but you may want to cite them. In the first case, these should be primary sources, and every effort should be made both to read them thoroughly and also to ask the kinds of questions above. In other words, they should be critically interrogated. Critically does not mean criticising them but subjecting them to the same level of methodological and theoretical scrutiny you would apply to your own research!

Meta-analyses and measurement

Analysis of findings in quantitative research is often conducted through *meta-analysis*, which is a method of summarising the results of a particular kind of quantitative review, especially one that has a distinct, easily measured outcome variable, such as the average statistical difference between the control and the treatment groups in experiments. These mean differences are usually stated in standard deviation units. Doing so means that they can be compared across studies and averaged across studies. Without standardisation, they cannot easily be compared or legitimately be statistically summarised. It is worth noting that the basic math involved in an elementary meta-analysis is remarkably simple. Indeed, when meta-analysis is applicable, there is no easier way to summarise groups of studies on a topic. That is because you can pool groups of outcomes, or compare them across groups, by using *standard deviation* scores.

This is an effective point to stress the centrality of the standard deviation, not only in meta-analysis but also as the basis of nearly all modern statistics. It is the foundation on which most of the rest is built. It is hard to think of a recipe for a statistical technique that is not founded on the standard deviation as a key ingredient. And the standard deviation is one of the few statistics that is definitely worth while knowing how to calculate by hand – just to make sure you know what it is. Most simply, the standard deviation is a measure of how much the scores in a group of scores differ from the average; it is the mean difference from the mean (see

Volume 3). A group of values with a high standard deviation would be more spread out than a group with a low standard deviation (*SD*). For example, if the average coat in a store cost €50, and the *SD* were €10, most of the coats would sell for between €40 and €60. But if the average were €50, and the *SD* were €100, the price range would be much broader.

Meta-analyses are valuable and indeed restricted to research where the same, or rather similar things, have been measured. One of us, for example, has used a measure of how close students or academics, in sociology, believe that discipline is to the arts/humanities or to the natural sciences (Williams et al., 2008). This measure, though not a perfect one, has been used in several studies now, allowing a standard deviation from the mean, across those various studies to be calculated. This in turn may (and indeed has) demonstrated a stronger effect, because not one but several samples could be compared. Though meta-analyses of this kind are more possible than might be supposed, in quantitative research, they are a subset of literature reviews in general. Nevertheless, when possible, they are a valuable basis for your own research, particularly as you may wish to replicate some or several measures from other studies into your own.

Replication is, in itself, an important strategy in social research (as in science more generally), but in practice in social research, it is not carried out nearly as much and is often a low-status activity that can struggle to attract funding. In social research, replication is harder than in the natural sciences, because there is much more variability in characteristics, attitudes and beliefs in the social world than the physical world. For example, measurements of temperature can be standardised anywhere in the world or at any time, whereas measures of social class are difficult to standardise across place and time. Measures of social class in the United States will work less well in (say) India or South Africa. But replication can be a valuable tool when a research strategy, or an instrument such as a questionnaire, can be validly applied in different times or places. This does not mean that one takes a questionnaire, originally used in Toronto, and administers it in Tokyo. Language issues aside, such a questionnaire would need to be tested for validity in the new location, before being applied (Litwin, 1995, pp. 59–69) to see whether respondents understood and answered the questions in the same way. An excellent example of the replication of a survey instrument across cultures can be found in the European Social Survey (see Jowell et al., 2007 and www.europeansocialsurvey.org/). A useful guideline for translating surveys in cross-cultural research can also be found at the Methods and Measurement Core at the University of California, San Francisco (http://medicine.ucsf.edu/cadc/cores/measurement/methods.html).

Replication does not have to be of a whole study. It might be the replication of a sampling strategy, or it might be just of a question/questions or a scale. Replicating a question or questions means that data from one study can be directly compared with data from another study. For example, a very simple measurement of whether students see sociology as closer to the arts/humanities or the natural sciences has been used across several UK studies of attitudes to quantitative methods. Although populations, the nature of the studies or the samples differ, asking the same question permits comparison. Sometimes this is done post hoc, where data from questions in several studies are harmonised. See, for example, the work undertaken at the Centre for Longitudinal Studies at University College, London, https://cls.ucl.ac.uk/new-harmonised-data-on-childhood-circumstances-now-available-to-researchers/.

Conclusion

Literature reviews can range from the very simple and informal to the detailed, rigorous and extensive. They may incorporate not only meta-analysis but also a range of different kinds of literature from the speculative, theoretical or qualitative to papers or reports that are based on extensive surveys or secondary analysis. When these are reported and described in the literature review of the paper, monograph or research report, how fully they are described is largely dependent upon both their centrality to the current research and what they themselves represent. One should be cautious not to extend the same epistemological authority to each item.

Thus, though one should aim to be methodical and scientific in conducting an analysis of prior literature and the studies, or theorising what these represent, it is something of an art as to how much and how one reports these. The foregoing is then not intended as a set of instructions but more as a guide on how to proceed.

Chapter Summary

- Nearly all research has a history! That history exists in previous research on a topic and research that might have important substantive or methodological links to your own research.
- This chapter is concerned with how you go about finding out about previous research through a literature review.
- The chapter describes how to go about this task and how to maximise its effectiveness.
- The final part of the chapter briefly describes the task of meta-analysis in which the results of previous research may be combined or reanalysed to produce more powerful findings.

Further Reading

Vogt, W. P. (2007). *Quantitative research methods for professionals*. Pearson.

The final chapter in this book brings together literature reviews, synthesising research and (a topic in the current volume's final chapter) assessing research quality. It also has an in-depth discussion of validity and reliability (see previous chapter).

Ridley, D. (2012). *The literature review: A step-by-step guide for students* (2nd ed.). Sage.

This is a clear and comprehensive guide to conducting literature reviews. It is illustrated with examples from a number of disciplines.

Several other guides to literature reviews can be found at https://uk.sagepub.com/en-gb/eur/disciplines/P16.

4

RESEARCH DESIGN AND RESEARCH RESOURCES

Chapter Overview

Introduction

In Chapter 2, we provided an overview of the structure of quantitative research by briefly discussing the role of theory and the structure of data into cases and variables. In Chapter 3, we discussed some of the necessary preliminary work that must be done through literature reviews and possibly meta-analyses of previous studies to help you find or develop theories that will inform how you do your research. We should, however, stress that these stages or processes are rarely linear, or simple, and most research requires an iterative backwards and forwards journey between the literature, the research question and the theory.

In this chapter, we will discuss matters of design and resources. It might be said that whilst **research design** is question led, it is resource driven. We will begin with design.

Design

Your research question will not determine, but will certainly inform, the design of your research. Design is not method but more to do with the logic of inquiry. The design chosen and the methods that arise from this will depend on what kind of research is being conducted.

What does it mean to design something? Suppose you are to build a new house from scratch. You would need a builder, a plumber, an electrician and so on. You would need to decide whether you build from wood, concrete, brick, prefabrication and so on. You may prioritise environmental features, storage, light and so on. But before you can decide these things, you need an architect to design the house, both its external appearance and how it is aligned and arranged internally. You need a design.

So it is with research. Just as you don't start from the assumption you will build wholly in brick, or you will have certain environmental features, you don't begin your research from the assumption that you will use a postal survey, or you will use a specific data set. Once you have your research question, or questions, you need to think about research design.

Let us begin with thinking a little more deeply about what it is we are doing in order to choose our design.

Description and explanation

In Chapter 2, we touched on the issue of description and explanation. This may be rephrased as *what* is going on and *why* is it going on? We also discussed types of theory, and it is these matters – what and why and whether we are constructing or testing a theory – that will inform design. We illustrate these things, for simplicity, with a hypothetical example. Suppose your interest lies in describing the labour market in a particular city. For example, who does which kind of jobs – men, women or particular ethnic minorities? What are their levels of education? Where do they live, and how far and how do they travel to work? What are the characteristics of the unemployed? How much sickness is there in the workforce? You are seeking descriptions of these things. But why? Well, it may be that an organisation or government department concerned with these things wishes to know more, in order to develop policies. Or it may be that you are testing particular theories about the composition of the workforce and how that may be different or similar to elsewhere. A very large amount of research is descriptive and is often a necessary stage in developing explanations, answering *why* questions.

Let us continue the analogous example: suppose in the city of interest there is a generally high employment rate but high unemployment amongst certain ethnic minorities and young people in general. If you are interested in answering this question, you have moved from a wish to describe to a wish to explain why employment patterns are unequal. Now, supposing you have a data set that has information on all, or most, of the key variables of interest; you may use a somewhat basic strategy of treating employment as the dependent variable and then performing a whole series of cross-tabulations with other independent variables to look for statistically significant effects. Now, we say this is basic (it may even be naive), but we should stress that there is nothing wrong with doing cross-tabulations per se, but there is a prior step and that is 'Is there a good theory (perhaps developed from research elsewhere) that may offer a possible explanation?' Such a theory may, for example, suggest that cities with poor tertiary education opportunities will have a skills shortage amongst groups finding it harder to access those opportunities. Thus, this middle-range theory is a starting point in your research and will lead to more sharply focussed analyses.

Explanations, then, are closely related to theories and provide the logical structure of a testable theory, which goes something like this: if we know that certain things hold, under particular known conditions (sometimes called the *explanans*), then if these conditions exist elsewhere, then those same things should be the case there (the *explanandum*). So that if in several similar cities, poor training opportunities – in the tertiary sector – have led to sectorial high unemployment, then we would propose that this would be the case in our example. There are three things to say about this: firstly, this, what is called the 'covering law model', is often much more untidy than the example might suggest (Williams, 2016, pp. 54–58). Secondly, rarely does the theory tested in specific circumstances yield exactly the same results, and it usually ends up being modified somewhat. Thirdly, the strategy of analysis we describe above would lead actually only to a fairly shallow explanation, but nevertheless one that might be fit for a purpose in particular circumstances.

Often, however, we are developing theory. In practice, this usually means that we have some informal hunches as to what is going on, or some kind of social problem that requires explanation. Developing theory and testing theory are iterative processes, and often researchers, in testing their theories, come to modify them. Developing theory may be via initial description, but qualitative research can also be a valuable tool. In our hypothetical example, then, we may begin with descriptions which will tell us how many people are like X or are doing Y. At this stage, we may use and then test prior theories, or if they are unavailable, we may develop our own from these descriptions, or try to flesh them out through qualitative work – perhaps through focus groups or depth interviews with key informants (see Flick, 2016).

A theory may, of course, be wholly descriptive, but this is unlikely and mostly not very interesting. Most theories are posited as answers to 'why' questions; they offer, if they were true, explanations of what is going on. In all of these, there is an elephant in the room. Most explanations are, at least implicitly, causal explanations.

Causal explanations

In Chapter 2, we attempted to give a feel for the complexity and diversity of causes. As we noted, causal explanations take many forms (Cartwright, 2003). Take, for example, poverty and life expectancy. How would we attempt to frame a causal explanation? There is plenty of evidence that in those areas of the UK that are 'poorer', the average life expectancy is considerably lower than in those areas that are better off. To say poverty causes early death is an attractive political slogan (or very unattractive if you are of opposite political persuasion), but as a scientific claim, it just won't do.

Firstly, some people in rich areas die early, and some people in poor areas live to a grand old age! So, any potential causal claim is based on a population mean. For dramatic effect, politicians often compare the two extremes (and these may indeed be atypical 'outliers'), and many locations will not show such dramatic differences.

Secondly, what is being measured when one speaks of 'poor' and 'rich' areas, and would alternative measurements produce different 'poor' and 'rich' areas? For example, one might use some or all of the following: unemployment, proportion of people on the minimum wage, the median wage, food poverty, housing quality, life expectancy, morbidity, access to private or public transport and educational attainment.

Thirdly, there are lots of intervening variables between being poor and dying early, and some of these may be more important than others in contributing to the net effect, which may moderate or mediate the effects. For example, is smoking a greater contributor than, say, stress?

There are plenty of other obstacles to a causal claim, but these give a flavour.

On observing the kind of effects, we describe, researchers often begin by trying to tell an informal story about what might be going on. This 'story' will more often than not be informed by prior theory, itself derived from examples elsewhere (hence, the *explanans* and the *explanandum*).

So let's tell a 'causal story'! The poor areas have high unemployment, and what employment there is, is low skilled and low paid. The opposite is the case in the rich areas. Unemployment and low wages lead to food poverty, but something else is going on. The poor area is a traditionally working-class area, with once-traditional divisions of labour and lifestyles that culturally and historically arose from these. Thus, things like poor diet and especially smoking are not wholly attributable to poverty. This is a simple, far too simple story, but cast your eye over it, and look at the things we would need to measure to turn the story into something more scientific.

In practice, most researchers do aim for causal explanations, but these are not simple ones, and the kind of causal explanations they aim for are those that come from probabilistic models. There will be a lot more of this in later volumes, but a simple model might go something like this:

Dependent variable = proportion of population dying 5 years younger than the national mean life expectancy.

Independent variables = employed/unemployed, manual/non-manual class, limiting long-term illness/or not, smoker or not, cancer registration, net earnings, weekly food spending, years lived in location and type of housing.

On the face of it, the independent variables look both intuitively appealing and fairly comprehensive. However, we would caution about making any causal claims without carefully assessing the potential joint effects (interactions) between key independent variables like the interrelationship between housing type and having a limiting long-term illness and reflecting upon our choice of variables. Are there omissions in our model? Do the data fail to cover important effects such as a person's life history of employment? Certainly, having access to good-quality **longitudinal data** for analysis allows us to examine the accumulation of periods of unemployment and assume that prior exposure to disadvantageous events leads to premature mortality. Whilst temporal ordering provides some comfort for those who wish to make causal inference, it is not enough on its own. There will always be the threat of omission or the presence of bidirectional influences – for example, being a smoker may result in a person having a limiting long-term illness, or having a limiting long-term illness may result in smoking (to ease anxiety or physical pain).

How much you worry about causality is often the result of your prior epistemo-logical position. Positivists, who are true believers in that creed, will not worry at all, because they will maintain that all we can ever show is statistical association (however complex) between variables. Realists are less dour than this, and whilst agreeing with Professor Cartwright (see Chapter 2), they nevertheless think causal explanation is a worthwhile goal. For their part, causal stories are often fleshed out into causal mechanisms (built up from the statistical models and with a bit of reasoning as to whether something is a plausible causal explanation). A causal mechanism is a complex array of interconnecting characteristics, which cohere together to produce particular outcomes. The aim of realist causal explanation is to model plausible mechanisms to explain effects (Williams, 2018).

And somewhere between the pessimistic positivists and the optimistic realists lies the previous subsection and the causal analysis tradition. On the whole, its adherents believe in models, but less so mechanisms, but frankly, it's often hard to tell them apart from the realists (see e.g. Blalock, 1961; Blau & Duncan, 1978; Rubin, 2008).

The search for meaning

No, not an existential diversion, but one to give due consideration to explanation's twin, or, indeed, its alter ego!

Max Weber's (1949) methodological maxim was that an explanation should be adequate at the level of cause and meaning. By this, he is usually understood to mean that when we offer an explanation of why something happened, that explanation is not adequate without an understanding of the meanings people gave to their behaviour or decisions that led to the outcomes we wish to explain. For example, in counter-urbanisation research, population movement from urban areas to rural or less urban areas can be well described through population statistics (Champion, 1994). We can, for example, come to know the occupations or professions of migrants, their level of education and the characteristics of origin and destination locations. From this we may, as many studies have, conclude that a significant group of migrants appear to improve their economic position upon migration and thus theorise that such migrants move for economic reasons. But there are exceptions, and occasionally, migrants do improve their economic prospects and may indeed move from wealthier urban areas to poorer non-urban areas (Williams & Champion, 1998). Why did they do that? Perhaps they made miscalculations about the prosperity of their destination or they moved for non-economic reasons, perhaps lifestyle ones.

To find these things out, as indeed counter-urbanisation researchers have, one needs to explore the *meanings* that migration had for the migrants. What reasons did they give and how did they come to these reasons? This is but one example (and it is provided because one of us has interests in this field), but virtually every research question that requires an explanation rather than a description invites an exploration of meaning. And just to spice things up a little more, can those meanings collectively build toward a social cause? We won't try to answer that, because it is beyond the scope of this book.

Meanings are often seen to be the province of qualitative research, and indeed, this is just what qualitative research is about, but quantitative researchers are capable of and very often do research meanings through their instruments (see Flick, 2016; Marsh, 1982).

This quick tour of description, explanation and meaning and their relationship to theory now brings us finally to the matter of design and how these things fit with different designs.

Types of design

Following David de Vaus (2001), we propose that there are four principal designs that may apply to both quantitative and qualitative methods. These may subdivide, are often combined or one may be embedded within another. Indeed, one of us (Vogt, 2007) has proposed eight different designs. However, for the sake of simplicity, these four will act as 'ideal types' for us to discuss some of the principles of design.

Whether you seek description, or explanation, or whether you are testing a theory, or developing a theory, the design chosen will have a bearing on the nature of data generated. Furthermore, though one design may recommend itself over others, there may be methodological, or resource, constraints on why this design cannot be used. We discuss the second of these at the end of the chapter. But now, an overview of the four designs.

Cross-sectional design

In the social sciences, the vast majority of research will use a cross-sectional design. This can look very different, depending on the methods used, but they all have one thing in common, the absence of a time dimension. That is, the data are collected at one time point. The methods may have involved surveys, collection of official statistics or even qualitative research. The data collection may be 'primary' – that is, a bespoke survey conducted (or say focus groups in qualitative research) to answer a specific question or questions – or the research may be based upon secondary data. The methodological considerations will be very different in primary or secondary research, but again a second thing they will have in common is that they can only measure differences between groups, not change. For sure, respondents' perceptions, or experiences of change, might be measured, but not actual change. Primarily, cross-sectional designs provide only description, and anything beyond that is usually informal inference.

However, repeated surveys of the same population may give some clues about change in that population, but because the members surveyed will likely be different, only the change at population (and possibly subpopulations) level can be inferred. These designs include repeat cross-sectional studies or continuous survey – for example, the Family Resources Survey, which provides annual information about the incomes and living circumstances of households and families in the UK (www.gov.uk/government/statistics/family-resources-survey-financial-year-201819). For much research, describing change at an aggregate level does not matter, but it places limitations when one wishes to move from description to explanation. Cross-sectional designs may provide explanations, in that they may show how phenomena are linked together. For example, in many societies, the educational level of parents can be a 'predictor' of that achieved by their children (and thus an important factor in social mobility; Erikson & Goldthorpe, 2010; Goldthorpe, 1985). We could say that the child's educational attainment is 'explained' by that of the parents, but this is a thin form of explanation and often applies to a majority, but not an overwhelming majority of people, and may be far less the case in place A than in place B. It certainly does not give us a cause. Just think about it. In what way did your mum or dad getting good grades in X subject cause you to get good (or bad) grades in X or Y subject? This is an example of the isomorphic nature of prediction and explanation; though a prediction might be inferred, it is nevertheless a weak form of explanation, because it derives only from associations, and generally cross-sectional designs can provide only associational explanations, not causal explanations.

Why is this? The first problem is that often when we wish to say one thing caused another ($A - B$), we measure A and B at the same time, and cause A must precede B. And we have measured A and B together. In the educational example, parents preceded children, so we can at least infer a link over time. In many areas of research, temporal precedence cannot be known. Take, for example, homelessness research. Homelessness and unemployment are strongly associated. But does unemployment cause homelessness, or the other way around? Actually, in practice, it is much more complex, with causality running in each direction, and even more difficult to provide causal explanation because of the heterogeneity of homelessness and the very temporal nature of forms of homelessness (Williams & Cheal, 2001). If you wish to attribute causality in homelessness, cross-sectional research may not be the best design.

Secondly, cross-sectional research must rely on measuring existing differences during a specific time period (often referred to as the period of fieldwork) in the sample. Changes in characteristics, behaviours, attitudes and beliefs will change over time at different rates in any given sample, so that the cumulation of these things contributes to the gradual formation of a causal mechanism.

Nevertheless, even in cross-sectional research, statistical controls and modelling can permit at least statistical inference that can eliminate some causes, or at least provide some evidence for causes. This will be discussed more fully in Volumes 9 and 10.

Case study design

Case studies are often also described as a method. Case studies are the gathering and analysis about one or a small number of examples as a way of studying a broader phenomenon. The assumption being that the case is typical of a broader phenomenon. Cases may be individuals, villages, factories, schools, friendship groups and so on. For example, a political scientist wishing to study why some candidates for public office are successful and others are not might study a particular election campaign in great depth in the hope of finding some general lessons about the electoral process. Case study research is often associated with qualitative methods, but this is certainly not exclusively true. For example, community studies, such as Wilson's (1997) study of the decline of traditional forms of employment in Chicago, may employ several methods, such as surveys, individual diaries or systematic observational research. Case studies achieve explanations by intensive analysis of many variables within a case (de Vaus, 2001, p. 249). In recent years, a small number of researchers have begun to do quantitative research that begins with the individual case (usually a person) – rather than variables – and then conducts analyses across cases using probability theory or Boolean logic to make generalisations (see the Byrne & Ragin, 2009, edited collection).

Case studies can have another valuable role, that of theory building. Admittedly this was often conducted using qualitative methods (and this is a book about quantitative methods). Continuing our hypothetical example, in order to develop a theoretical explanation of why certain ethnic minorities suffer higher levels of unemployment, we may conduct some life history interviews with a few 'cases' – members of an ethnic group of interest. Thus, our research may employ two initial designs: (1) cross-sectional or (2) case study.

In building theory from case studies, we employ a particular form of inductive reasoning. The assumption upon studying a 'case' is that she, he or it will exhibit features typical of a population. Though inductive, this is not the same as the more formal probabilistic reasoning employed in **probability sampling** (see Chapter 5 and Volume 3). This form of reasoning is informal, what one of us has termed *moderatum generalisation* (Williams, 2000). So, for example, our interviews of ethnic minority members indicate specific forms of discrimination: we might hypothesise that this might be the case in the wider group. But we can test this hypothesis. In good research, it would not be lightly derived. Just saying that such discrimination was experienced would not be enough. The research would probe to discover where, how many times and how the discrimination had been manifested, before this became operationalised as a measure in a survey.

Experimental design

Causal explanation is the raison d'être of experiments. The following is a very brief overview of the design itself, because experimental method is the topic of Volume 6.

Experiments were initially developed in the physical sciences (physics and chemistry). In this, they embodied the classic covering law model in which a phenomenon could be tested, in laboratory conditions, according to known laws. For example, the rate of cooling of an object can be deduced from the measured properties of that object, consistent with a known law – in this case, the second law of thermodynamics. Laboratory experiments, then, begin with a hypothesis derived from a body of theory, or law. In the laboratory, all extraneous influences are controlled for (or at least those that are known) and an operation is performed. The experiment is an active intervention by the scientist and not simply a passive observation of nature.

But the world outside of the laboratory contains phenomena with uncountable and often unknowable properties. Thus, in social science research, and research more generally in the social world, different experimental strategies must be employed.

The first of these attempts to overcome the problem of the messiness of the social world through randomisation. This approach has become known as the randomised controlled trial (or RCT) and is widely used in clinical trials. In this, the probabilistic selection of cases into either an experimental or a control group is the substitute for the physical manipulation attainable in the laboratory. Let us assume a drug company has developed a drug to reduce blood cholesterol. After initial trials (often with animals) to test its safety, a sample from a target population, suffering from high cholesterol levels, will be selected (there may be prior stratification by age, sex, body mass etc.). The sample is (say) 2000. One thousand will be randomly assigned to the experimental group and 1000 to the control group. The trials are usually conducted 'blind' with the subjects not knowing whether they are in the control or experimental group. Each will be administered a pill, under the same conditions, with the same dosage and so on, but those in the control group will receive a placebo. At the end of the trial, the success of the treatment will be measured. The tests (in this case) might be the amount of blood cholesterol present before and after treatment. Rarely will a successful trial show a uniformly positive effect in the experimental group, and often a proportion of the control group will show positive results. What counts as a successful[i]

---

[i]What counts as 'success' can be substantive or methodological. Substantive success would be a positive effect in the experimental group, but methodological success could be an unambiguous positive or negative finding.

trial will depend on a number of things, such as the magnitude of the findings or whether they are statistically significant. These issues have been the subject of debate in recent years, particularly the issue of 'statistical significance' (see Volume 3).

Whilst RCTs can be used and are used in social research, the 'treatment' administered is much more difficult to control than a simple pill. Assume, for example, one wishes to test support strategies for return to work for the long-term unemployed. In principle, straightforward. Again, say 2000 unemployed people with similar characteristics are identified as a suitable sample. One thousand are randomly selected to participate in the 'back-to-work' scheme (the experimental group) and 1000 become the control group. Each is compared for (say) employment outcomes over a 6-month period.

What could possibly go wrong? The programme either works and most/all of the experimental group are in work, or it does not, and there is not much difference with the control group. But what if

- the 'treatment' of the back–to-work scheme is operated slightly differently across the experimental group?
- some members of the experimental group drop out of the scheme?
- some members of the control group use other strategies to find jobs?
- a whole lot of new jobs are created in the area, benefitting both groups?
- those in the experimental and control groups start talking to each other and this changes their approach to seeking work?
- more than one of the above operates simultaneously?

Finally, in open systems, most confounding factors are psychological or social. One of the most important of these is the 'placebo effect', which refers to a psychologically induced (usually positive) change in those in the control group who believe that the 'treatment', in fact a placebo, is having an effect on them. A famous variant of this, in a social setting, is known as the Hawthorne effect. This refers to a series of productivity experiments conducted in the Hawthorne Plant of the Western Electric Company, in Chicago, in the 1920s and 1930s (Adair, 1984), and it demonstrated that social effects over time were crucial factors in production and these often outweighed any physical changes in working conditions introduced by the experimenter.

The foregoing is not an attempt to put the reader off experiments. Many of the above effects (sometimes called violations of assumptions) can be controlled for. Indeed, Volume 6, demonstrates how social researchers might successfully overcome these difficulties.

But there is another, quite widely used, strategy – that of the quasi-experiment, in which the members of the experimental and the control groups are not randomly selected but are selected on the basis of known characteristics. One of us conducted a classroom experiment in which those students taking particular modules (course) in two universities were taught an enhanced range of quantitative methods. The control group were all the other students in the year group who had not taken the modules. This provided two experimental and two control groups, allowing for a four-way comparison (Williams et al., 2016). It has to be said that the results were equivocal, with some indication of better performance and more positive attitudes in the experimental groups but not wholly so. Indeed, the data from one of the universities was badly compromised by a high dropout rate in the experimental group.

But these difficulties can be overcome to a great extent through replication of the experiment with other groups over time. Thus, it is possible to see whether the small observed effects get bigger, with more samples, or were perhaps an aberration in the original research.

We have spent a little more time on experimental design, which may seem rather odd at first sight because it is perhaps the least used of the four main designs. However, the logic of the experiment extends to other designs.

Essentially, experiments depend on manipulation but are achieved through intervention. In studies of human populations, it is often impossible to randomly assign individuals to treatments or exposures simply because you cannot actively manipulate where someone lives. The absence of a physical comparison or control group mean that contrasts (comparing 'like with like') have to be achieved statistically. A good example would be the evaluation of the impact of environmental noise upon residents' mental health (Tarnopolsky et al., 1978; Tarnopolsky & Morton-Williams, 1980). These studies fall under the heading of quasi-experiments. William Trochim, a mentee of Campbell (Campbell & Stanley, 1963), informs us that Duncan Campbell used to refer to these experiments as 'queasy' because they gave experimental purists a queasy feeling (see https://conjointly.com/kb/quasi-experimental-design/)! But equally, longitudinal and cross-sectional designs manipulate data post hoc but do not 'intervene' through treatments. An increasingly popular statistical matching technique that attempts to achieve matching across comparison groups was introduced in the 1980s by Rosenbaum and Rubin (1983) and is known as 'propensity score matching'. For a useful account, see Oakes and Johnson (2006). There will be more to follow in Volumes 6, 7 and 8. In longitudinal design, much the same things happen, but the changes in variables are measured over time.

Longitudinal design

Quantitative longitudinal designs primarily use survey method. Many are large sample surveys that are repeated at regular intervals. Like cross-sectional designs, they can be used to describe or predict, but their strength lies in their ability to produce causal explanations. In doing this, they have one great advantage over cross-sectional designs – that temporal order can be established.

There has been an increased use of longitudinal design in recent years, particularly in the UK, because the resources in the form of large-scale and complex data sets have been prioritised for funding by the Economic and Social Research Council (ESRC). There are several longitudinal designs and combinations of these. We summarise the two main ones here.

Panel designs

The first and commonest of these is the prospective panel design. In this, a sample is selected (the panel) at one time point and data collected from them, and the same exercise is repeated with the same sample at a later time point. What is important is that these are the same people who are being followed through time. This is a central feature of a longitudinal study that contains repeat measurements on the same person over time and distinguishes a longitudinal study from a continuous survey. However, one of the issues with this design is that we cannot really know whether the measurements at each time capture real change in what is being measured, or whether intervening factors were responsible for more complex change. For example, in England and Wales, the Office for National Statistics holds more than half a million linked individual records for a 1% sample of individuals selected from the 1971 Census and followed in 1981, 1991, 2001 and 2011. However, the censuses are 10 years apart. So, for example, we can measure limiting long-term illness at each census (first measured in 1991) and say a person reports the same condition in 2001, but we cannot say whether this is the same condition at both times, or whether they had it throughout the period (Collett et al., 2006). The obvious way to overcome this problem is to take measurements at closer time points to allow the measurement of long-term and short-term effects and when these occurred.

One of the issues researchers must face, in panel designs, is that of replacement. People drop out of panels for all sorts of reasons – moving home, not wishing to participate any more, getting sick, dying and so on. So if one has measured at four time points, should one include those cases that dropped out after 1, 2 or 3 measurements? If those who were not measured at all time points are excluded, this presents problems of validity in the remaining sample. For example, if the focus of interest is health issues, those dropping out may have got sick or died of their illness.

So if replacements are sought, these are matched as closely as possible to the existing panel sample, but quite obviously there is no data for them at all of the time points, and they too may distort eventual findings. Over time, replacement panels will be increasingly composed of different individuals to those initially selected.

Some sophisticated (and it must be said expensive) studies will select overlapping or rotating panels. In this design, a series of panels is established and begin at different times;

so, for example, panel 1 might be sampled in years 1, 3, 5 and 7 and panel 2 in years 2, 4, 6 and 8. The same data are collected from each of the panels. A fine instance of ingenuity in design applies to the US Current Population Survey, which uses a 4–8–4 rotation system in which 75% of the sample is common month to month and 50% year on year (www.census.gov/programs-surveys/cps.html).

Cohort designs

The UK, in particular, has a number of excellent cohort studies. These are often based upon sampling people born on particular dates, or within particular periods. Some examples of these include the UK's National Survey of Health and Development study of a nationally representative cohort of people born in 1946 at the start of the 'baby boomers' generation. They have been followed since birth and are now aged 74 years (www.nshd.mrc.ac.uk). A more recent birth cohort study now aged 19 years is the Millennium Cohort Study, sometimes referred to as 'Generation Z' or 'children of the new century' (https://cls.ucl.ac.uk/cls-studies/millennium-cohort-study/). In Chapter 7, we will describe aspects of **data management** using the National Child Development Survey, when the cohort members were aged 50 years, which is another cohort study managed by the Centre for Longitudinal Studies at University College London's Social Research Institute. These data are made public via the UK's Data Service website (http://ukdataservice.ac.uk). The richness of the data quality makes it possible to follow the various journeys of cohort study members through their life course, and in some cases there are also data on family or household members. For a useful introduction to cohort or cohort study designs, see Setia (2016).

Cohort designs are particularly prone to the problem of attrition, but also one cannot be sure whether observed change is a cohort effect specific to those born at the same time, an ageing effect or a broader phenomenon due to the historical period in which the data were collected (e.g. see Blanchard et al., 1977). Some cohort studies mitigate these problems by selecting 'waves' or 'sweeps' of people born on later dates, or time periods, creating a multiple cohort design (e.g. the Longitudinal Aging Study of Amsterdam, www.lasa-vu.nl/lasa-introduction.htm).

Mixing designs

The four designs we set out here, we must reiterate, are ideal types. Most research will mix designs, often in imaginative ways and usually for practical reasons. Designs may run consecutively to test different aspects of theory, or alongside each other, or they may be embedded one inside another; so, for example, a case study design, where the 'case' is not an individual, but a workplace, a school or a village, may have longitudinal or experimental elements, within the 'case' (de Vaus, 2001). In clinical research (but as yet not in social research), a concept of '*n* of 1' is receiving attention. In this, a single individual is a 'case', and over time a number of experimental interventions, or observations, may be made (see e.g. www.bmj.com/content/348/bmj.g2674).

Methods and designs

As we noted above, there is no necessary link between design and method, but conversely some designs are more likely to lead to particular methods and some methods are associated with particular designs. In Chapter 6, we will look in more detail at types of method; so although in the next section we refer to particular methods, this is only to consider their resource implications.

Resources

Our research designs are ideal types, and any good researcher, given enough time, enough expertise and labour power can optimise design and the methods that flow from it. But there is a trade-off. To conduct an experiment, whether it is an RCT or a quasi-experiment, you need access to an adequately sized experimental and control group and you need a good idea that the people in each will stay the course of the experiment, otherwise your key resource of experimental participants becomes a diminishing one!

Resources, then, are not just money, they can be time, equipment, access, skills, expertise and respondents/participants. When we read a research report or article, the resources constraints are rarely mentioned, but even in the best resourced projects, there will be limitations. We do not hear, for example, that 195 people were interviewed because that's all there was time for or that multivariate analysis was not used because the researcher hadn't got that far in the SPSS book!

We are not suggesting that research is usually cheap and dirty, some certainly is, but a lot of research makes excellent use of the resources available. Here are some examples of resource implications that need to be considered.

The 'cheapest' research is often said to be secondary analysis of existing data and indeed, it is true, this avoids expensive data collection, the need to use interviewers and the subsequent data entry cleaning and coding, but it does require a skill set in the use of secondary data and access to the appropriate data set (more of this in Chapter 7 and Volume 5).

Longitudinal research is usually the most expensive design. Fortunately, most longitudinal research uses existing data from curated data sets and (apart from specific skills needed) has the same resource implications as secondary analysis. But mounting your own longitudinal research can be very resource intensive, especially in respect of time. Even (say) within a PhD, the maximum practical time period that can elapse between sweeps of data collection is around 1 year. Outside of PhD research, it is very hard to get longitudinal research funded, because of time and cost constraints.

For the researcher, early in their career or new to quantitative research, who is not undertaking secondary analysis, the method of choice is usually the survey. So, what are the particular resource issues with the survey?

- The kind of sample you would like to achieve, its size or accessibility may be an important factor. Sometimes there are methodological problems in achieving a desirable sample, but it can also be an issue of time available or access. We will say much more about the kind of samples that are desriable and sampling decisions in the next chapter.
- When the decision is made to conduct a survey, the inevitable question is self-completion or interview schedule? If the former, will it be online, and if so, how will the sample be achieved and participants contacted? As we will describe below, the research question will inform the design chosen, but some designs (like methods) are more resource intensive. A longitudinal design that requires primary research will, at least, require a period of time to make at least two contacts with the 'panel' of participants. Additionally, the researcher must be engaged upon the project long enough to make at least two contacts (and probably paid!). Then, there are the costs of conducting the survey in the field. So, a cross-sectional design may have to do if the resources are unavailable.
- If this is the case, then the cross-sectional survey may be given more 'power' through replicating measures already used in previous surveys of similar populations (see Chapter 2).
- Increasingly, researchers are using the internet for surveys. Most of these web surveys are self-completion surveys (Callegaro et al., 2015; Couper, 2008). A large number of people can be reached quickly, but the quality and sample representativeness of the contact may be poor. Moreover, internet surveys have especially poor response rates and often suffer from systematic non-response and/or item non-response (see Chapter 7).
- Interviews take longer and can be both of higher quality and explore topics in greater depth. But interviews take time to conduct and time to travel too. Respondents must be contacted and agree to interview. All of this takes time and money. On the other hand, a postal survey, used much less these days, will take many weeks. Respondents need time to reply, and further follow-up mail-outs must be made. If the research is to be done quickly, then, in terms of time, interviews will be quicker.
- Open-ended questions are expensive compared to closed (fixed choice) questions, and some market research companies charge clients a premium for each. Generally speaking, the simpler a survey, the quicker and cheaper it is. Open-ended questions have implications for time. If you are interested in in-depth opinions of a particular subset of the sample, then it is better perhaps to consider a simple survey and follow up using qualitative depth interviews.

- When designing the survey, consider that you or someone else has got to analyse it, and even with new versions of SPSS, STATA or R, the data have to be entered and 'cleaned', variables defined and labelled and so on. Once the tables start rolling out, they have to be interpreted. Don't ask more than you can analyse, but also be careful to ask all you will need![ii]
- However, many people reading this and the other volumes in the series will be conducting secondary analyses on large data sets. We have mentioned the methodological advantages and disadvantages of this in Chapter 2, but although many data sets are readily available, the time required to complete a thoroughgoing analysis can be considerably longer than one might imagine. Variables must be recoded, new ones created, imputations made and possibly data sets merged. These things are rarely straightforward and will often throw up anomalies and puzzles that take time to resolve.

These do not exhaust resource questions by any means but perhaps give a flavour of how to tackle them. Most importantly, these things must be costed for money, time and material resources. For example, if one is using interview schedules, try to work out how long each interview will take, consider travelling and contact time. How long will (say) the 300 interviews cost in person days, and how much does an interviewer cost per day? Above all, it is good survey practice to pre-test your **questionnaire design** and pilot your questionnaire (akin to a 'dress rehearsal', see an excellent account of good practice at the Pew Research Center, www.pewresearch.org/methods/u-s-survey-research/questionnaire-design/). Also, remember interviewers often need to make more than one call at an address before they are able to make contact with the respondent. How many interviewers can be afforded? In most studies, labour costs of researchers, interviewers and clerical staff will account for two-thirds to three-quarters of the total budget (see entry 'survey costs', https://methods.sagepub.com/reference/encyclopedia-of-survey-research-methods/n564.xml and Lavrakas, 2008).

This is also true if you are a 'lone researcher', maybe an undergraduate or a PhD researcher. You may not cost your time in pounds, euros or dollars, but your fieldwork must be completed in a timely fashion in order to complete your degree requirements in the allotted time. Primary longitudinal studies are technically possible but are far from being the most viable option. Face-to-face interviews must all be done yourself. Increasingly, 'lone researchers' are using either the internet to contact respondents or secondary data.

So before considering your design and your methods, consider the resources you have available both to conduct the study, if it's primary, and to analyse the data.

[ii]Unless you anticipate returning to further analysis at a later date.

Conclusion

This chapter has considered some of the most basic issues that a researcher faces at the beginning of the research process. The design of your research, cross-sectional, case study, experimental, longitudinal or hybrid designs, will to a great extent shape the kinds of descriptions or explanations that you can obtain. Design is logically independent of method but should always be prior to method. Much of this chapter has been written from the perspective that you, as the researcher, will be choosing your design to conduct primary research, but even if you are conducting secondary analyses, the design of the research that provided your data set will determine what kind of analyses you can conduct. The most obvious difference is between cross-sectional and longitudinal designs. The former have no time element in their data collection – they are just snapshots, so even though variables such as poor health and unemployment may be measured, it is hard to know which came first. In longitudinal design, such time ordering is often possible.

All research depends on resources, and the resources available may well determine both your design and your methodological choices. Mostly people think of money as the most important resource to fund a study, but as we have shown, other things such as time are crucial. The decision to conduct secondary analysis, for example, will often be on the realisation that it would be impossible to collect original data on several thousand people in just a few weeks, whereas a judicious analysis of existing data may well reveal results quite quickly.

Chapter Summary

- This chapter is concerned with two key matters in social research: that of design and research resources. The first of these is the underlying logic of research, that of the design to be adopted.
- Design is the architecture or framework of the research, and it makes a difference to the kinds of descriptions or explanations your research can arrive at, and therefore, the methodological decisions that must be made.
- We describe the four key designs – (1) cross-sectional, (2) case study, (3) experimental and (4) longitudinal – and how these designs may be combined.
- The possibilities and limitations of research are related to the available resources, things such as available time, available person power, the existence of sampling frames and/or available data, for secondary analysis.

Further Reading

de Vaus, D. A. (2001). *Research design in social research*. Sage.

The basic four-design model, illustrated in this chapter, is taken from David de Vaus's book. In this book, de Vaus discussed, in depth, the logic of research design and how these designs can apply in practice.

Vogt, W. P., Gardner, D., & Haaffele, L (2012). *When to use what research design*. Guilford Press.

As with de Vaus's book, this one emphasises the importance of the logic of design to research, but it also suggests a wider portfolio of designs and links these to methodological issues.

Tarling, R. (2006). *Managing social research*. Routledge.

There are not many books that discuss the resources you need to conduct and manage research, but Tarling's book is very detailed in this, covering topics such as commission and funding research, project planning and research staff.

5

SAMPLING

Chapter Overview

Introduction: generalising and sampling

Everyday life hinges on the practice of taking a sample, whether it be the first taste of coffee in the morning, the results of a blood test, the decision to move into a new flat or last night's culinary experience at the local tapas bar. We take the process of sampling as both necessary and sufficient for our very existence without being formal or overly scientific about the value of the first sip, taste, clinical result, purchase or food consumption. Over time, with the benefit of experience we come to trust the dish, product or decision to remain loyal to a particular restaurant, cafe or holiday destination. This is based on inductive reasoning, whereby we generalise our experiences from one time or place to another. We assume an excellent pizza eaten at one branch of a chain of restaurants will be just as good in another branch. The more pizzas we eat at different branches, that are deemed excellent, strengthens our belief.

And so it is with social research, we use inductive reasoning from a sample to make generalisations more widely.

Generalisation or generalisability is an important concept used by social researchers; the first term is used to indicate an important feature of science (and therefore social research), the ability to say whether findings from one study can be generalised to other populations and settings. The second term is used to assess how much or how well this is done, though the terms are often used interchangeably. In the natural sciences, generalisations are often grounded in laws, which all things being equal, will operate universally. In the social world, there is too much variability across communities, or through time, to allow the level of generalisation possible in the natural world. So, generalisation in social research can be of the informal kind, rather like in everyday life, where an inductive statement that social features in one place or time are deemed likely to be similar in others. These 'moderatum' generalisations are primarily propositional or the domain of qualitative research (Williams, 2000). In quantitative research, generalisations are statistical and based on reasoning from sample to population. For an excellent account of the importance of random sampling, see Bellhouse (1988). In selecting the sample and designing the research, the aim is to maximise external validity. This goes somewhat beyond not only generalising from sample to population but also whether and to what extent can various aspects of a study – for example, the proposed theory, the instrument, its format and questions within it – have the same meaning in other contexts.

In this chapter we want to introduce you specifically to sampling, to help you put sampling in the context of research design and subsequent analysis. It is primarily a summary overview, because sampling is discussed in more detail in Volume 4.

The *Cambridge International Dictionary of English* (Cambridge University Press, 1995): offers three definitions of sampling. The following comes pretty close to what we mean by survey research:

> A group of people or things that is chosen out of a larger number and is asked questions or tested in order to get information about the larger group.

Sampling is often seen as a difficult concept by new social researchers, but there are only two types of sample: probability (or random) and non-probability (though each divides into other techniques). The former is the 'gold standard' in social research, but it is not always possible, yet always to be desired! Consequently, most of this chapter is aimed at guiding you through some of the key principles and techniques of probability sampling. But at the end of the chapter, we will briefly describe non-probability sampling.

What is probability sampling?

In a probability sample, each member of the population has a known and calculable chance of being selected. The term *population* does not necessarily have to apply to the human population of a given geographical location, but it is a statistical term that refers to a collection of persons, groups, events or things about which we wish to generalise. Our population might be all of the people, or all of the adults living in Lewisham, south-east London, UK. It could be individuals, households, all of the police officers or the kebab shops. However, when selecting a sample from a population, always the intention is that the sample should be representative.

Suppose that it is the households that we are interested in, these become our target population, and then we must determine a sample size that will represent the target population. In quantitative language, 'big N' refers to the population size and 'little n' to the size of the sample. Thus, our definition of population is the 'target' of any statistical inference that we may make on the basis of a single sample. Secondly, for the sample to have any validity it needs to be more than a small part of the whole but an amount of elements (individuals, organisations, animals etc.) which have a *known and calculable chance of being selected* or included in our sample. This immediately raises two key practical challenges for any sampling exercise, namely, to identify and access an up-to-date list of our target population from which to actually draw our sample. This list is referred to as the *sampling frame*. The extent to which our sampling frame fails to include all members of our target population gives rise to *non-coverage error*. For example, if we were planning to survey voters from the electoral roll, we would need to be sure that all voters who are eligible to vote in any forthcoming election are actually registered to vote and are on the roll. It is well known that young men and the very old in the UK are under-represented on the electoral register. It is fair to say, of course, that it is unlikely that any sampling frame will be a perfect match for our target population and we have to have ways and means of extending the coverage in practice before deciding to live with the deficiencies in the frame.[i] The second challenge follows the completion of the sample design. Put another way, there should be a plan of making the sample selection which may endeavour to overcome deficiencies in the completeness of the available sampling frame. The design may have other features, like dividing the list prior to sample selection by region (known as *strata*) and selecting aggregates of the population within region like voting constituencies (known as *clusters*) prior to the final selection of individuals. To this extent, sample design starts to become an art form.

The second practical challenge to obtaining your desired sample size whatever means of data collection you decide to use (e.g. *face-to-face interviewing*) will be the willingness of the sample member to co-operate. Lack of co-operation generates a level of *non-response*. A person can simply refuse to participate at all or only answer certain questions (*item non-response*). Alternatively, the selected person may be out every time the interviewer attempts to conduct her interview. Non-coverage and non-response are generic terms for *bias*, which will threaten the validity of our inference. We may be able to remedy or fix some of the deficiencies in our coverage by design; but however elegant our sampling design appears in the office, it will be undermined by non-response bias. But, all is not lost. By and large, fieldwork (throwback term from 'going out into the field' to survey the world) survey agencies will put in enormous effort, including the use of incentives and repeated attempts to persuade the sample member to participate, to secure a sample of size '*n*' in order to reduce the impact of non-response. Sampling practitioners often draw a distinction between their *desired sample* size and the actual size of the sample obtained, the *achieved sample* size. In an ideal world, they should be the same, but in practice with response rates for general population surveys varying between 20% and 70%, sample designers have to build in strategies to boost their achieved samples. There are also statistical strategies that can be adopted to handle item non-response once the survey questions are answered and coded in a data file for analysis.

We say a little more about these strategies in Chapter 7, and the reader is encouraged to consult Volume 4, if they want to learn more about sampling and survey research methods. To continue, we will focus upon the importance of having a probability sample in order to build up an exposition of the theory of sampling and options for sample design. All these considerations will be important to quantitative researchers whether

---

[i] There have been regular methodological checks on the quality of the UK Electoral Register as a sampling frame. See Foster (1993).

you are designing and implementing your own survey (*primary data collection*) or analysing an existing (*secondary data*) survey.

Conceptualising a framework to evaluate your sample survey

We have already introduced two key sources of bias in sample surveys, namely, non-coverage and non-response errors. The other source of error is what we term *variable error*. This typically arises from sampling. Imagine that equipped with our sampling frame we selected several samples of a given size from our population list. The membership of any resulting sample will vary for samples of a given size from the target population. Whilst in practice our analysis will depend on a single sample, there is an underlying theory that captures the concept of sampling variability, and this is a major source of variance in our statistical analysis. Other components might include the differential effect that interviewers have on the propensity of sample members to provide accurate answers to their questions; for example, some interviewers may systematically prejudge the attitudes or values of bearded men or tattooed ladies. Put together, the components of bias and variance for any given survey question can be combined to define the *total survey error* and following Kish (1965) can be presented schematically. The construction of Figure 5.1 depends upon knowledge of Pythagoras's theorem in that the square of the length of the hypotenuse is equal to the sum of squares of the lengths of the other two sides of the right-angled triangle. In Kish's original diagram, variable error is made up of sampling and fieldwork. Sampling triangles refer to how many stages of selection contribute to the design and fieldwork to the various dimensions of data collection and processing (referred to as data entry or coding in the days before computer-assisted survey methodology). Contributions to bias are principally those described as non-coverage and non-response. The quantitative distinction between bias and variable error is that bias cannot be eliminated however big your little 'n' becomes, whereas variable error can be reduced by increasing your sample size. Put another way, the larger the part of the whole you select, the more likely it is that any sample estimate based on the sample will approach the population statistic you are hoping to capture. We will demonstrate this later. Combining bias (indeed its square) and variable error (a variance which is already a square) is called the *total survey error*. Kish's diagram reveals a conceptual means for evaluating your sample.

A moment's reflection of course and you'll say, 'ah, but these elegant triangles only apply to a single survey question, so the concept of total survey error will be different for different questions'. Of course, but like most things that come to test our search to assess just how our survey results are, survey statisticians like Kish himself have come up with statistical approaches to handle the fact that surveys will typically be

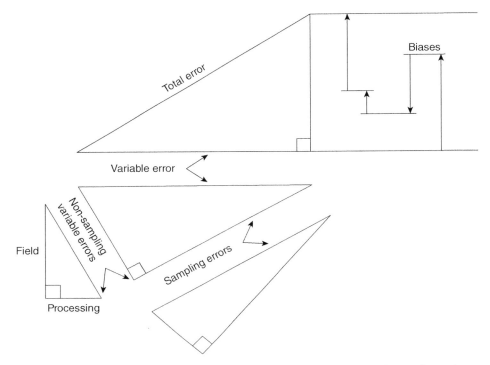

Figure 5.1 A conceptual framework for evaluating survey biases and error based on Kish (1965)

multi-item in content and multipurpose in nature. The conceptual model presented in Figure 5.1 can be generalised so that survey practitioners can begin to evaluate their surveys and answer grand questions like 'how can I optimise my sample design for a given outlay of resources?' but now let's return to basics and outline the process of making generalisable statements based on our achieved sample.

What do we mean by a random sample?

We have already emphasised the importance of probability samples which convey a known and calculable chance of selecting someone (an element) from our target population but how do we achieve this selection? The lottery would be a fine analogy where unique numbered tickets are placed into a drum and spun to mix them up. Five lucky numbers are chosen by placing a hand in the drum; each time a selection is made, the ticket is placed on a table and not returned to the drum. This is prob-ability sampling *without replacement*. Its opposite, *sampling with replacement,* would be to return each selected ticket to the drum and restart the process. This distinction is important from the point of view of developing sampling theory but not necessarily for achieving a sample of five distinct lucky numbers. Under the first scenario, let's imagine there were 50 tickets in the drum; the first ticket would have a probability of 1 in 50 of being selected, the second 1 in 49, the third 1 in 48 and so on. We have achieved our sample of winning tickets knowing the probability of selecting each ticket and we have done so in a fair and transparent manner provided the person selecting the lucky ticket each time cannot see or read the ticket in advance (e.g. they may have a subconscious preference for odd numbers).

In practice, when our target populations are large and we have access to a suitable sampling frame, we need to arrange our list so that individuals have a unique identifier or number for selection purposes. Our list may be inherited from a particular source like a voter register, so we need to know if the list has any properties that may affect our sample selection. For example, if the list is ordered alphabetically taking a sample at random using the lottery analogy may produce a sample in which all share surnames beginning with 'Z', which may in turn result in an over-representation of certain minority ethnic groups. The sample would still be random according to the principles of haphazard selection, but we might manage the sample membership in a manner which avoids any inherent biases in the ordering of the list. The remedy is to adopt a scheme known as *systematic random sampling*. Consider a list which uniquely identifies our target population where $N = 1000$ and we wish to sample 1 in 10, that is, $n = 100$. Each individual will have 1 chance in 10 of being included in the final sample where n/N represents the *sampling fraction* – here 10/100 which equals 1 in 10, of course. In most textbooks on survey sampling (e.g. Groves et al., 2009), the sampling fraction is labelled as f (for fraction). The inverse of f or N/n gives us the *sampling interval* here 10, which is the step from converting the sampling fraction into the means of proceeding to select a systematic random sample from our list. What the process enacts is a division of the original list into 100 blocks of 10 individuals. We begin by selecting a random number between 1 and 10 and successively add 10 to our *random start* to loop down the list selecting one element from every block. Random numbers can be generated by computer algorithms or in sampling days of old a set of random number tables to be found at the back of a lot of classic textbooks. Figure 5.2 illustrates the process for a random start of number 2 on our list, someone with the surname (given) of Azan. In practice, our sampling lists will not have nice divisible population sizes like 1000 to provide us with whole number sampling intervals, but you will be pleased to know that there are ways around such matters (see how to handle fractional sampling intervals in Kish, 1965; Groves et al., 2009).

Thus far, the sample size has been treated as a 'given' or a 'fixed' number like 100. Again, in practice the constraints on our sample size will often be resources (a combination of time, effort and money) although for a given budget the art of sampling means that we can deviate from having to rely solely on a systematic random sample

Unique ID	Name	Selection
1	Arnold	
2	Azan	**2 = our random start between 1 to 10**
3	Asquith	
....		
100	Bijal	
101	Cookson	
102	Cramer	**Second selection**
....		
200	Duval	
201	Drucker	
202	Ernesto	**Third selection**
....		
902	Zaha	**Final selection**
.....1000	Zygota	

Figure 5.2   An illustration of systematic random selection

and use existing information about the sampling frame like knowing not only the person's name but their street address and postcode. In this way, we can *stratify* the list in advance and select our sample by region or postcode sector. It is not only convenient to spread our sample geographically, but it may help us provide *survey estimates* that provide important information about how our population varies across the country – for example, levels of poverty by region, the level of voter intention to vote for a particular political party at the next national election. Before we can do this more exciting stuff, we need to know some more about how we can go about determining the sample size in advance with a little help from the statistical theorists. First, we will begin with some properties of simple random samples and the resulting survey estimates (arithmetic means and proportions in this instance), then proceed with an illustration of how we approach the determination of sample size from a theoretical basis.

Probability samples are the gateway to statistical inference

A key concept in the development of statistical inference or how to make generalisations about the characteristics of our target population based on those obtained from our sample is the *sampling distribution of sample statistics for samples of a given size and, indeed, the properties of the distribution (its shape and spread)*. We need to appreciate these ideas largely because in the everyday practice of doing statistics and, in particular, estimation, they are somewhat hidden from view or taken for granted. A bit like the 'light bulb' metaphor, you don't need to know much about electricity in order to turn the light on; however, in your case, it might be informative to have some appreciation of how the statistical world contributes to quantitative research (a bit like knowing how to change a fuse). The basic idea underlying statistical inference when we want to *estimate* something about our population of interest is that we draw upon a law and a powerful theorem referred to as the 'law of large numbers' and the 'central limit theorem' (Feller, 2008; Haigh, 2012). The former enables us to make reliable statements about a population value based upon a single small (random) sample of values. The latter is quite amazing and allows us to make inferential statements about our survey statistics with a known level of confidence (typically, with 95% or 99% confidence where a 100% would represent certainty). This is made possible when we have a relatively large sample and the knowledge that whatever the shape or form of the distribution of our sample statistic (e.g. the mean), the sample mean will be approximately normally distributed (bell-shape, symmetrical and centred on the population mean). For more detail, Volumes 2 and 3.

In this section, we are going to provide an appreciation of some key ideas in statistics by using a few numbers. The approach is based on an elegant monograph on scientific sampling by Alan Stuart (Stuart, 1964) without the assistance of much technology other than a calculator. The illustrations that follow are based upon a *simple random sample*.

To trivialise the real world, consider a population consisting of four individuals: Azan, Bertrand, Collette and Dagmar (labelled A, B, C and D, respectively, for convenience). Imagine that we already know the values of certain key characteristics for each person in advance, for example, their age in years. Table 5.1 contains these ages and the average age of the population (the mean).

Table 5.1   The ages (in years) of a hypothetical population where $N = 4$

Azan	Bertrand	Collette	Dagmar	Mean Age of Population
28	39	21	44	33

Suppose you decide to select two individuals from this population at random using a lottery method. How many potential samples are there if we adopt sampling without replacement? Pause for thought and close your eyes. Yes, the answer is six. Now suppose each sample is equally likely as a contender for being the one that represents the population and you want to estimate the population mean age based on your sample? Appealing to your reasonable self, it would appear logical to use the sample mean to estimate the population mean. Table 5.2 lists all possible samples of size 2 from a population size 4 and provides the resulting sample mean in each case:

Table 5.2 An illustration of a sampling distribution of sample means for all possible samples of size 2 from a population size 4

Sample Members	Ages (in Years)	Sample Mean
1. A and B	28, 39	33.5
2. A and C	28, 21	24.5
3. A and D	28, 44	36.0
4. B and C	39, 21	30.0
5. B and D	39, 44	41.5
6. C and D	21, 44	32.5

If any one of our six samples had an equal chance of being the sole sample used to represent the population (we could achieve this by rolling a six-sided die to designate exactly which one), then the survey estimates of the mean age would vary between 24.5 and 41.5[ii] years. Indeed, none of our sample estimates would actually coincide with the true underlying population mean (of 33 years). However, the mean of the sample means would do (check for yourself)! What this illustration has demonstrated so far is that the sampling distribution of sample means for all possible samples of size 2 selected from a population of size 4 has a mean equal to the population mean. This is a simple way to demonstrate what statisticians imply when they describe the survey estimate as being *unbiased*. What we also witness is that the estimates will vary and the 'good news' is that we can quantify this variation (soon). Before doing so, let's see what happens if we consider increasing our sample size to 3. A moment's thought reveals that there can only be four possible samples of size 3 from 4 (see Table 5.3).

Table 5.3 An illustration of a sampling distribution of sample means for all possible samples of size 3 from a population size 4

Sample Members	Ages (in Years)	Sample Mean
1. A, B and C	28, 39, 21	29.33
2. A, B and D	28, 39, 44	37.00
3. A, C and D	28, 21, 44	31.00
4. B, C and D	39, 21, 44	34.67

[ii]In this illustration, all of the estimates are unique and, therefore, have a frequency of 1. For large populations and selected samples, the distribution would begin to look familiar with some estimates appearing more than once.

Remarkably, the mean of the sample means for all possible samples of size 3 from 4 is again exactly equal to the population mean. The range is now narrower 29.33 to 37.0 than when the sample size was 2. Indeed, this demonstrates an important finding that by increasing the sample size by one person, we have a *more precise* estimate of the population mean. Precise in the sense that we have background information based on the empirical properties of the sampling distribution of means that the range becomes narrower as your sample size gets bigger. Taken to an extreme when $n = N$ (= 4), there is only one sample (equivalent to a census of all population members) and consequently no variation in the estimate of the population mean. The range is a very quick and ready estimate of any variation in our sample means to obtain. But its width can be affected by extreme outlying values of the minimum and maximum, so in general we find that the *standard deviation* is preferred as a means to convey the concept of precision in statistics. In colloquial terms, this is a measure of 'how far on average any value (in a distribution) is from the average'. Trying to translate this expression into a number is tricky. Look what happens if we subtract the population mean from each value in our population and try to average the differences. Before we consider that action, it is important to calculate each distance from the mean (also referred to as a deviation) in the same way, so any value below the mean has a minus sign in front and conversely any value above the mean a plus sign (see Table 5.4).

Table 5.4 Developing a measure of variation for a population ($N = 4$)

Individual	Value (Age in Years)	Distance From the Population Mean
A	28	28 − 33 = −5 (5 years below the mean)
B	39	39 − 33 = +6 (6 years above the mean)
C	21	21 − 33 = −12 (12 years below the mean)
D	44	44 − 33 = +11 (11 years above the mean)
Average distance from the mean = Sum of distances/4 = 0/4 = 0		

Our clever idea of trying to quantify how far on average a value is from the population falls flat when we try to average how far we are from the average because the sum of the distances equals zero. This will be the case for any set of numbers. How can we get round the problem? One solution is to ignore the plus and minus signs and simply calculate the average of the absolute distances, here = 8.5 (34/4). This measure is called the mean deviation, and it carries with it the argument that we are not so much interested in averaging the distances whilst taking '+' or '−' signs into account but the total amount of departure from the mean itself. Another solution and one favoured by mathematical statisticians is to square each distance, add the sum of squares then average and to approximate back into the original measurement scale and finally take the square root. Table 5.5 shows the result.

Table 5.5 Calculating the population standard deviation

Member	Value (Age in Years)	Deviation	Squared Deviation
A	28	−5	25
B	39	+6	36
C	21	−12	144
D	44	+11	121
Total sum of squared deviations			326
Average of sum			81.5
Square root of average sum			9.03

The average of the sum of squared deviations (81.5) is called the population *variance*. Its square root, the value 9.03, is the population *standard deviation*. It is close but not equal to the mean deviation. An example of how often in quantitative research there is more than one way of operationalising (putting a number to) a concept. Any characteristic like the mean or standard deviation describes the properties of a distribution of a variable (age). Here the mean represents a 'typical' person or position on the distribution (formally the mean is referred to as a measure of location). Pause for a moment and consider the variance of the sample means in Table 5.2 reproduced in Table 5.6.

Table 5.6 Sampling variance of sample means for samples of size 2 from a population size 4

Sample Members	Ages (in Years)	Sample Mean	Deviation From the Mean (33.0)	Squared Deviation
1. A and B	28, 39	33.5	0.5	0.25
2. A and C	28, 21	24.5	−8.5	72.25
3. A and D	28, 44	36.0	3.0	9.00
4. B and C	39, 21	30.0	−3.0	9.00
5. B and D	39, 44	41.5	−8.5	72.25
6. C and D	21, 44	32.5	−0.5	0.25
Total sum of squared deviations				163
Average sum of squared deviations (variance of sample means)				163/6 = 27.16[a]

[a]Later shown to be equal to the population variance × $1/n \times (N - n)/(N - 1) = 81.5 \times 1/2 \times 2/3 = 27.16$.

There is a connection between the population variance and the variance of the sample means. The former describes variation between the individual values in the population, whereas the latter describes the variation between the sample means based on samples of a given size (here 2). Intuitively, you might expect more variability in the population than in summary statistics based on samples drawn from the population. It turns out that if you multiply the population variance by $1/n \times \{(N - n)/(N - 1)\}$ this is exactly equal to the sample variance of the sample mean $[81.5 \times 1/2 \times \{(4 - 2)/(4 - 1)\}] = 81.5 \times 1/3 = 27.16$. Apart from the extreme case when a sample becomes a complete enumeration or census where $n = N$, this connection holds for samples of any size.

For populations, these characteristics are constant (even if they are unknown in most instances), whereas their corresponding estimates based on a sample survey will vary depending on the composition of the sample membership. Expressed as generic terms, this distinguishes the *parameter* (based on the population) from the *statistic* (based on the sample). Putting algebraic labels on our two parameters, we usually find the Greek letter μ (mu) for the population mean, σ (sigma) for the population standard deviation and σ^2 for the population variance. The corresponding sample statistics are typically labelled $\bar{x}$, s and s^2. Always remember of course that in writing about statistics and labelling characteristics, we don't have to always stick to convention just like Humpty Dumpty in Alice in Wonderland; we can choose words (and letters) to mean anything we want them to mean. In that way, $\bar{x}$ is more than a label – it is a symbol for a variable that summarises the operation of adding values and dividing the resulting total by the sample size. When we want to estimate a population parameter using a sample statistic, we would like it to be *unbiased* or in statistical terms speak for its *expected value* to be equal to the population parameter (something like knowing that for all possible sample means from a population the mean of the sample means is equal to the population mean). Indeed, it works beautifully for the sample mean. As Stuart (1964) affirms, the 'correspondence principle' suggests that when we are estimating the population mean 'what can possibly be better than to calculate the corresponding function (the average) in the sample?' He calls this the 'correspondence principle'. But the same outcome does not hold for the population variance where the 'mirror' or 'corresponding' calculation for the sampling distribution of sample variances does not produce an unbiased estimate of the population variance. The failure of this principle to do the same for the unbiased estimation of the population variance led statisticians to remedy the deficiency. It turns out that if we divide the total sum of squared deviations by $N - 1$ for the population and similarly for each of the sample sum of squared deviations describing the sampling distribution divide the sum of squared deviations by $n - 1$, then the sampling variance of the sample means is equal to the population variance multiplied by $1/n(1 - f)$, where f, our friend the sampling fraction, equals n/N. Of course, for large-scale surveys n may well consist of several thousand individuals selected from a target population of several million and the adjustment $(1 - f)$ becomes so close to 1 that we can safely ignore the correction and simply divide the population variance by n.

In our examples above for all possible samples of size 2 from 4 (Tables 5.1 and 5.2), $1 - f = 1 - 2/4 = 0.5$, which is not negligibly different from 1 at all; neither, of course, would 0.25 when $n = 3$ from 4. Let's see if it works for the first case in Table 5.2. This time we are going to calculate the sample variance for each possible sample using the 'old approach' and divide the sum of squared deviations by 2 each time and then simply adjust the estimate and divide by 1 instead (see Table 5.7), which is equivalent to multiplying the sample variances below by a factor of n/(n–1) (= 2, here).

Table 5.7 Calculating the sampling variance for the sampling distribution for all possible samples of size 2 from a population size 4

Sample Members	Ages (in Years)	Sample Mean	Sample Variance	Adjusted Sample Variances
1. A and B	28, 39	33.5	30.25	60.50
2. A and C	28, 21	24.5	12.25	25.50
3. A and D	28, 44	36.0	64	128
4. B and C	39, 21	30.0	81	162
5. B and D	39, 44	41.5	6.25	12.50
6. C and D	21, 44	32.5	132.25	264.50
Total of variances			326	652
Average of sample variances			54.33	108.67

Note. For samples with two values, the sample variance is simply the difference between the values squared and divided by 4, for example, for sample 6 the sample variance $= 1/4 \times (44 - 21)^2 = 1/4 \times 529 = 132.25$, and so on.

The adjusted population variance in Table 5.5 is $326/3 = 108.67$, which as if by magic is equal to the average of the adjusted sampling variances (also 108.67); so we have an unbiased estimate of the population variance.

These results are very powerful, and quite apart from providing some insight into the world of statistical theory, they tell us that in practice when we are only working with a single sample drawn from a specified population that in addition to being able to estimate the population mean with an unbiased estimator (the sample mean), we have learned that this mean will be a representative of a range of possible means for which (in theory) we can also estimate the sampling variation around that sample mean. Up until this point, we have set up the illustrations by assuming that we know the population values in advance so we have been able to demonstrate important links between our sample and the population. In practice, we have to have a remedy to do something to provide a handle to the likely 'error' around our estimate. For known values, we have defined the sample variance of sample means to be equal to the population variance times $1/n \times (1 - f)$ – only we don't know the population variance. We do know that it's possible to obtain an unbiased estimate of this parameter by using a sampling variance estimator, but again that depends on knowing the sampling distribution of the sample means. What we actually end up doing is using the sample variance based on our survey sample. To remind ourselves that the resulting standard deviation refers to our knowledge of a sampling distribution of sample means, we call this estimate the 'STANDARD ERROR'. So, provided our sample is large the standard error becomes $\sigma / \sqrt{n}$ or strictly $s / \sqrt{n}$ – a rather simple algebraic signifier which carries a considerable amount of background information. Its equivalent for variables which are dichotomous (e.g. Republican supporter or not amongst a sample of US residents) reduces to $\sqrt{P(1-P)/n}$, where P stands for the proportion of supporters in the population for which we can substitute the sample proportion (p) from our sample as our estimate of P. We have discussed the concept of unbiasedness and sampling variation in this section. Now, in order to make generalisations about population characteristics, we need to know a little more about the actual distribution of the sample means. One approach would be to just use the sample mean as an estimate of the population mean, but what we have learned is that sample means vary despite the fact that on average they are centred at the population mean. We capture the extent of this variation in our estimate of the standard error so it would be wise to use this information somehow in the construction of our estimate. We are going to build some informed caution into our estimation about the shape and properties of the sampling distribution. This caution gives rise to what you may have heard of as a *confidence interval*. Just how confident or cautious we want to be is our decision, but typically, we adopt conventions like being 95% confident that the interval estimate contains the population mean.

Being able to generalise with caution or confidence?

To reiterate what we said in the opening paragraphs of this chapter, the aim of sampling is to be able to generalise. Generalising is easy, but generalising with confidence that your generalisation will hold requires the construction of a confidence interval estimate. This section describes how to do that. Essentially we add and subtract a quantity from our sample mean. This quantity is referred to as the MARGIN OF ERROR for an estimate of a population mean or proportion.

The form of the confidence interval = sample mean ±margin of error,

where the margin of error = A multiplier times the standard error.

The value of the multiplier articulates the level of confidence we desire and is selected from the properties of a famous distribution called the normal distribution (or if preferred the Gaussian distribution). So do we carry out the calculation of an estimated confidence interval?

The arithmetic builds upon a massive mathematical theorem in statistics, that we mentioned above, called the *central limit theorem*, which provides a powerful result that tells us that whatever the shape of the population distribution of a variable, the resulting shape of a sampling distribution of sample means for samples of a given size will be symmetrical and centred on the population mean; that is, the axis of symmetry is a line which divides the distribution exactly into two halves with 50% of the sample means below the axis and 50% of the values above. Put another way, the population mean is also the middle-most value along the distribution (called the median) and its height (relative frequency) at that point is at a maximum (the mode); that is, for symmetrical bell-shaped curves, the mean, the median and the mode are all equal. Whatever the shape of the population distribution from which we are drawing our sample, the resulting sampling distribution of means (or proportions as a special case of a mean) will approximate the normal distribution. You may be interested in estimating average income or wealth (housing stock, investments etc.), which is known to be *skewed* or non-symmetrical because the high-end values of income and/or wealth stretch the tail of the distribution. But you can build upon your sample estimate together with a margin of error in the knowledge that the sampling distribution of average income or wealth will be normally distributed. Once we can assume that any measure is normally distributed, we only need to know two things (parameters if you prefer) about the measure – its mean and standard deviation. Because we are in the business of estimation, you may recall that the standard deviation of the sampling distribution of means is synonymous with the standard error. A general property of the normal distribution is that by moving three standard deviations either side of the mean you cover 99.9% of all values. In the case of the sampling distribution of sample means this translates as by travelling 3 standard errors either side of the mean and you will have covered almost 99.9% of the range of values that capture the range of possible sample mean estimates. Table 5.8 provides two conventional values of the multiplier (taken from the standard normal distribution) for varying levels of confidence.

Table 5.8 Values of the multiplier for varying levels of confidence

	Level of Confidence	
	95%	99%
Multiplier	±1.96	±2.58

Note. The multipliers are equivalent to the number of standard deviations (here errors) along the horizontal axis of the normal distribution that you have to travel either side of the mean to cover 95% or 99% of all possible values of the sample mean. There will be more reference to the normal distribution in Volume 3.

For the purposes of illustration, suppose that we have conducted a study of the local labour market with an achieved sample of 1440 and obtain a sample mean of £34,000 with a sample standard deviation of £12,000.

A 95% confidence interval for the mean income would be

$34,000 \pm 1.96 \times 12,000/\sqrt{1440}$

$= 34,000 \pm 1.96 \times 316.23$

$= 34,000 \pm 619.81$

$= £33,380.19$ to £34,619.81

If we want to feel more confident about the estimated confidence interval and we raise our confidence to 99%, we would obtain an interval of

$34,000 \pm 2.58 \times 316.23$

$= 34,000 \pm 815.87$

$= £33,184.13$ to £34,815.87

In a nutshell, if you want to be more confident about your estimate, you simply make the interval wider by increasing the value of the multiplier as we have shown. However, you have to draw the line somewhere. Ideally, you might prefer certainty, but then the width of the interval would be so wide that it would be pointless going to all that trouble to mount a survey in the first place. The interval estimates above seem pretty plausible but another way of narrowing the width of the interval would have been to opt for a bigger sample (say double the size to 2880) and stick with the conventional 95% confidence interval. Assuming that the sample mean and standard deviation remain the same, then the estimate would be

$34,000 \pm 1.96 \times 12,000/\sqrt{2880}$

$= 34,000 \pm 223.61$

$= £33,776.39$ to £34,223.61

The simple 'take-home message' is that by increasing the sample size, your estimate will be more *precise* in that the standard error will be smaller, but because the standard error is a function of the square root of the sample size, in order to halve the value of the standard error, you would have to increase the sample size by a factor of 4 (since, $\sqrt{4} = 2$). This would not be a realistic option if you are working to a fixed budget.

Determining sample size and allocating your sample

Once we have an understanding of the principles which underlie the production of a confidence interval estimate for a given sample, we are also able to use the formulae to answer a different question of our survey sample, namely, *how big a sample do I need to achieve a desired level of precision in my estimation?* It is not quite so straightforward to say 'the bigger the sample, the better', as the exact precision depends on the nature of the sample, the number of variables used to describe the sample and indeed the resources you have (de Vaus, 2014). The law of large numbers means that a small sample of a large population can sometimes better describe that population than a large sample of a small population. We therefore need a way of calculating an appropriate sample size. For example, let's say that we wanted to know the sample size necessary to be able to estimate the mean annual income for workers in our local district to within £2000? Put another way, this translates as setting the margin of error to £2000, then

$$2000 = 1.96 \times s/\sqrt{n}$$

Assuming our level of confidence to be 95% (i.e. set the multiplier to 1.96) and the survey estimate of '*s*' to be £12,000 from a past survey. Then by squaring both sides of the expression to rid ourselves of the $\sqrt{}$ we obtain

$$n = \{1.96^2 \times 12,000^2\}/(2000)^2$$

$$= \{3.8416 \times 144,000,000\}/(4,000,000)$$

$$= 3.8416 \times 36$$

$$= 138$$

Quite a modest sample size but then we are assumed to be content with a fairly wide margin of error. Let's try another example involving proportions. Assume that we wanted to estimate the proportion (or percentage) of adults living in Mauritius who wanted their government to actively encourage islanders not to dispose plastic waste in the sea to within 2 percentage points? How big a sample would we require? Remember that the formula for the standard deviation of a proportion simplifies to $\sqrt{P(1-P)}$, which is written as $\sqrt{P(100-P)}$, when *P* is a percentage. Of course, *P* is unknown and the objective of our survey, but luckily the properties of $P(100-P)$ can be anticipated. Take a look at Table 5.9.

Table 5.9 Selected values of $P \times (100 - P)$, where *P* is a population percentage

P	10%	30%	50%	70%	90%
100 − P	90%	70%	50%	30%	10%
P × (100 − P)	900	2100	2500	2100	900

Note that the maximum value of $\sqrt{P(100-P)}$ is when $P = 50\%$ so that in cases where we do not have an estimate P from any previous survey as the example for the mean above we can take the 'worst-case scenario' view of the world and assume that P is 50%, which will imply that the standard error will be at a maximum for any given sample size. Thus, using the expression for the margin of error for 95% confidence interval estimate,

$$2\% = 1.96 \times \sqrt{P(100-P)} / \sqrt{n}$$

$$n = \{1.96^2 \times P(100-P)\}/2^2$$

Now inserting $P = 50\%$, we get

$$n = \{3.8416 \times 2500\}/4$$

$$= 2401$$

Provided all of sample residents in Mauritius respond to our survey, a sample of just over 2400 sounds reasonable and not likely to break the bank.

Up until now, our arguments have rested on the idea of having a simple random sample (or indeed, a systematic random sample) to create our statistical description of the social world and learn about a few useful things like how to be cautious in our estimation and determine the sample size when planning a survey. However, in practice, we may want to depart from simple random sampling (SRS). We have already mentioned the idea of stratification when there is additional available information in our sampling frame other than names, addresses, contact telephone numbers or email addresses – for instance, region or gender which enable the sample design to allocate the sample across the groups or strata defined by the characteristic at the outset and sample systematically within each stratum. It may be convenient to do so but also desirable if survey sponsors would like key estimates by region or gender. If it so happens that our stratifying variable is related to the key variable of interest in our survey, like income, then we will gain in precision; that is, the resulting standard error will be smaller than if we had ignored the opportunity to stratify (more about this in Volume 4). In general terms, a departure from SRS in our design will have a consequence for the precision of our estimates. SRS is, if you like, a 'bench marker' for probability sample designs. Let's briefly consider some of these issues.

Departures from SRS: the consequences of design for sample allocation and estimation

Firstly, before we describe the various departures from SRS, let's continue with the application of stratification. In practice, a decision has to be made about how to allocate the sample across the various strata before sample selection commences. One of the most obvious ways of doing this is to allocate the sample in proportion to the population, so if 40% of the adults in a particular country live in the northern-most region, then we will allocate 40% of the sample to that region and sample at random (most likely using systematic random sampling) within each region. Without generating a lot of algebra, this design can achieve an equal probability sample for every member (labelled EPSEM) provided you sample at the same rate in each stratum. Thus, if the overall sampling fraction is f, where $f = n/N$, then the sampling rate in any stratum S will be n_s/N_s set to be equal to n/N. The opposite of *proportionate allocation* is unsurprisingly described as *disproportionate allocation*, where we decide to allocate a disproportionate amount of our sample in one or more strata. Colloquially, this is referred to as 'oversampling' or 'undersampling'. Its use does not imply that we have departed from probability sampling, but the change in the rate of sampling within a stratum would mean that we would have to 'weight' the resulting stratum estimates to balance the difference in the probabilities of selection in order to obtain an estimate for the sample as a whole. This is quite straightforward to achieve with modern software tools, but it is best to have a good reason for departing from proportional allocation. It may be that you have a substantive reason to study the residents of particular region in greater depth than other regions, or it could be that the costs of sending out interviewers to far-flung places may deter you from using proportional allocation. There are other theoretical reasons too like knowing that your key survey variable varies considerably within strata and that would lead you to oversampling the more variable strata.

The thing about stratification is that the sample literally visits or picks up sample members from every stratum. In a way, a stratified design comes closest to our understanding of having a *representative* sample. There can be more than one stratifying factor in a design provided the individual membership of the strata is known in advance.

Alternatively, we may know that individuals are in aggregates known as clusters, such as polling districts, aeroplanes or buses full of passengers or schools with classes full of pupils. We no longer sample every cluster but select a sample of clusters before sampling individuals within a selected cluster. If we sampled every cluster in our population, then the cluster would no longer be a cluster but a stratum. The point about cluster sampling is that it will typically involve two or more stages of selection so for that reason the term is often used interchangeably with the term *multistage* sampling. An important attraction of cluster sampling especially when you are conducting face-to-face interviews or computer-assisted surveys involving interviewers is to manage the allocation of your sample so as to select a fixed number of interviews (referred to as a 'workload') at the second or final stage of selection. For a two-stage design, first-stage units or clusters are selected with 'probability proportional to size' or *pps* so that the relatively bigger clusters receive a relatively greater chance of being selected compared to smaller clusters. At the second stage, a constant or fixed number of sample units (typically people or addresses) are selected within the selected first-stage units. Cleverly, as if inspired, the product of the two selection probabilities known as the *overall probability of selection* is always constant.[iii] An EPSEM sample is nicely designed so that the allocation of the sample is not going to spread out all over the country, thereby saving travel and fieldwork management costs. For more about the delights of sampling and probability laws, see Volume 3.

Design factor

A lot of what we have presented so far hangs off the form of a confidence interval estimate or in particular the 'margin of error', which has two major components: the multiplier (determined by your level of confidence) and the standard error (the ratio of the population standard deviation, or an estimate thereof, to the square root of the sample size). The magnitude of the standard error is determined by your sample design (classically, a simple random sample) and the sample size (either inherited in the case of secondary analysis or chosen as a result of your budget in the case of primary data collection). In practice, sample designs do not have to hinge on being a simple random sample. There can be departures for good reason, notably stratified random samples and cluster samples or indeed a combination of the two features. There are two important points to emphasise here about departures from SRS: you can still achieve a probability sample where every member of the sample has a known and calculable chance of being selected (more about probabilities of selection in Volume 3) and the magnitude of the standard error (the square root of the sampling variance) is affected by the nature of the sample design. Typically, for stratified random samples, for samples of the same size the standard error is smaller than that of one based on an equivalent SRS, and conversely, the standard error is larger than that of one based on an equivalent SRS for a cluster sample. Under stratification, you are using prior information so if the stratifying factor (e.g. region) is related to your key survey outcome, you gain in precision (smaller standard error, all other things being equal). Under a clustered design, it is likely that members of the same cluster (residents of a household) have similar views and habits so there may well be a duplication of information if your sample contains more than one cluster member. This brings about an inflation in the sampling variance, so our estimate will be less precise, all other things being equal.

[iii]Formally, the overall selection probability = (number of *psus* to be sampled) * (*psu* size)/total population size * (fixed number of interviews per selected *psu*)/(*psu* size). The numerator (*psu* size) of the first-stage selection probability is equal to the denominator of the second-stage selection probability leaving a constant overall selection probability whatever *psu* is selected.

These are rather sweeping generalisations, but they do have import from sampling theory and enable us to think of departures from SRS in terms of a quantity called the *design factor*, which equals the ratio of the standard error under the actual or adopted sample design to its equivalent assuming SRS, that is,

Design factor (*deft*) = $SE_{Actual\ design}/SE_{SRS}$

If the standard error based on the actual design is equivalent to one based on SRS then, of course, *deft* = 1. Typically, *deft* < 1 for stratified designs and *deft* > 1 for clustered designs. A stratified cluster design could lead to *deft* hovering around 1. The value of *deft* can be applied in the construction of a confidence interval making the interval width narrower or larger depending upon the design. A related measure to *deft* is *deft²*, commonly called the *design effect* (*deff*). This measure is used when we are considering sampling variance, which turns out to be related to costing models and concepts like sampling efficiency. Firstly, *the effective sample size* (*neff*) of any design refers to the size of a simple random sample that would achieve the same level of precision as your actual sample size (*n*), where

neff = *n*/*deff*

Thus, for any *deff* < 1 you are going to gain in efficiency (effective sample size bigger than the one actually achieved), and vice versa for any *deff* > 1. Numerically, for *n* = 2400 and a survey variable with a *deft* = 1.3, *neff* = 2400/1.3² = 1420. The ratio of *neff*/*n* expressed as a percentage gives us a measure of sampling efficiency here, 1420/2400 × 100% = 59%, which is another way of saying that our actual sample is equivalent to a simple random sample with 1420 sample members. Our sample efficiency is 59% compared to a simple random sample.

Non-probability sampling

The methods of non-probability sampling are very much simpler than the above, but frankly the confidence in the ability to generalise from sample to population is much weaker. Resources, or the absence of, or the accessibility to, a sampling frame can necessitate the adoption of non-probability samples.

Quota sampling

Quota sampling might be seen as 'the next best thing' to probability sampling and even has at least one methodological advantage over probability sampling! In the past, the debate over the science of 'probability sampling with quotas' (Sudman, 1966) versus probability sampling has largely divided market researchers from academic and government statisticians (Marsh & Scarborough, 1990). The former have defended the methodological practicality and accuracy of quota samples.

A quota sample requires the researcher to know how many people (or groups etc.) there are in a given population with the characteristics of interest. Often the basis for this prior knowledge comes from national censuses or other population measures. In any given town or city (in the UK, USA and most other Western countries), we can find out how many men and women there are, how many in each age group, how many live in public housing, how many have access to cars and so on. Consequently, we can design a sample where a quota is proportionate to the number of people with that characteristic in the population.

But it does have some drawbacks. Commonly, it is used by market researchers to undertake face-to-face interviews, typically in shopping centres or malls. For example, whilst an interviewer (the interviewer actually makes the selection according to the quota) can quickly fulfil a quota in a busy shopping centre (on the basis of age, sex, social class etc.), there may be peculiarities about such people not specified in the quota characteristics. For example, though eventually you might fulfil your quota of those people in manual social classes, it may well be that the shopping centre/mall chosen is too expensive to attract many people from those classes, which means those you eventually sampled may be atypical, because they over-represent that group as shoppers in that centre or mall.

Secondly, some characteristics, especially age, depend on an initial observation selection. If you need five people between 40 and 50 years of age, it is quicker to go for those who 'look' about 45 years. Again, you will fulfil your quota, but within an age range, the selection may be narrow.

But there is one advantage! Provided you persevere long enough, the problem of non-response goes away!

Sampling rare and elusive populations

Another key departure from the rigours of probability sampling occurs at the very outset of our attempts to select a sample simply because the target population is rare or 'hidden' and constitutes a minority. A 'rare' population is one where there are a few within a larger more general population, for example, piano tuners or Esperanto speakers, whereas an elusive population is one that is wholly or partially hidden, say marijuana users. A rare and hidden population will combine both traits. Consequently, there is no neatly available sampling frame of our population of interest. In some instances, an existing survey might provide a subsample of our population of interest, for example, lonely older people, provided we can obtain access to the data in order to identify the older and the lonely and carry out follow-up or in-depth interviews.

Mostly, however, in these circumstances, we must have recourse to snowball samples, where one respondent can be an informant and lead to other members of a population, or simply a convenience sample where one recruits any available respondents. In recent years, snowball sampling has been improved upon by a technique called respondent-driven sampling (Heckathorn, 1997). The size of rare and elusive populations is measured by estimating individual probabilities of selection in order to provide some reliable generalisations (Bernard et al., 2018), or capture–recapture, where observations of some proportion of a population are used to estimate its overall size and characteristics (Sudman & Cowan, 1988; Williams & Cheal, 2001).

Conclusion

In this chapter, we began from the simple but important notion of generalisation. To be able to generalise is crucial in social research, and rigorous sampling is therefore essential. Much of the chapter has been concerned with an introduction to some of the key characteristics and techniques of probability sampling.

We began this with describing an overarching framework for considering the major threats to measurement – principally, bias and variance. We then continued to focus on the availability of a suitable sampling frame and the construction of a confidence interval estimate for a mean and a proportion based on SRS and, more latterly, the impact of departures from SRS.[iv] All of these considerations have rested upon the generation of a single statistic from a single sample survey when we are all too aware that large social surveys or opinion polls produce information for several questions. Put simply, our information needs are typically multipurpose and therefore require many items in order to enhance our knowledge and understanding of the various aspects of the social world – for example, national studies of sexual behaviour (Erens et al., 2014) or crime victimisation (Office of National Statistics, 2017). Whatever your survey topic, the numbers you end up analysing will be generated by a complex process involving many prior decisions about how to collect the data, definitions and plain old 'human error'. None of this complexity

---

[iv]For those interested in knowing more about the practicalities of **survey design**, see Czaja and Blair (2005) and for those interested in the calculation of standard errors for complex survey designs, see Greenaway and Russ (2016) who have produced a helpful guide (with wide application) to assist users of the UK's Office of National Statistics social surveys (www.ons.gov.uk), which includes illustrations of ways and means of accounting for survey design in SAS, R, SPSS and STATA.

should prevent you from adopting a conceptual framework which provides a systematic way of thinking about the quality of your survey whether it be one that you have downloaded from a data archive for secondary analysis (see Volume 5) or one in which you have been involved as a contributor to the sample design and analysis (Volumes 2, 3 and 9). It is important to remember that in primary survey research, no matter how much effort you have put into the construction of a sampling frame and your sample design and whatever mode of data collection you have decided upon, you still have to implement the sample selection and secure those respondents in order to realise the benefits of probability sampling. Achieving a response will typically mean arranging for repeated callbacks (to the sampled address, telephone dialling, reminder emails etc.). If people refuse to cooperate, then it will be helpful to record as much information about the non-responders as possible in order to address the problem of differential non-response and so on. If your survey data is archival, then it is still important to access as much information about the survey process as you can (sometimes called *paradata*, like how many attempts were made in order to obtain a response).

Beyond the practical challenges of actually securing a probability sample, this chapter has largely ignored any discussion of the interplay of survey costs and precision, which will, of course, be a major consideration in how you use your budget or evaluate the worth of your information stock (see Chapter 4).

Our focus in this chapter has been to draw your attention to the importance of knowing more about the process of generating numbers (data) so that the numbers represent 'information'. In Chapter 7, we will connect the value of the information generated by the survey process with the importance of having an analytical strategy to make best use of the information at your disposal and preparing your data carefully to meet those objectives. It is important to remember that your sample design will have implications for your analysis. This may well be in terms of any reweighting of the data or adopting statistical procedures which explicitly handle your design features. In particular, the application of a statistical modelling technique which explicitly handles cluster samples is explained in Volume 9. In the next chapter, we deal with the creation of data in the context of the survey. Meanwhile, we leave you with a quote from Karl Popper:

> The history of science, like the history of all human ideas, is a history of irresponsible dreams, of obstinacy, and of error. But science is one of the very few human activities – perhaps the only one – in which errors are systematically criticised and fairly often, in time, corrected. This is why we can say in science, we often learn from our mistakes, and why we can speak clearly and sensibly about making progress there.
>
> – From *Conjectures and Refutations: the Growth of Scientific Knowledge* by Karl Popper (1968)

> **Chapter Summary**

- The data that are derived from a sample are the culmination of a complex process of decisions, available funding, the availability of a suitable list to sample from, the sample size to be achieved, the mechanism of selection to use, the mode of data collection and the effort required to secure cooperation from the selected sample members.
- Taken together, these aspects will inform our ability to make generalisable statements about the population of interest.
- This chapter introduces the theory and practice of sample design and evaluation.

Further Reading

Forsberg, O. J. (2020). Polls and the US presidential election: Real or fake? *Significance, 17*(5), 6–7.

Moon, N. (1999). *Opinion polls: History, theory and practice (political analyses).* Manchester University Press.

At the time of writing, the US Election polls report that Biden has an 8.5% lead over Trump (UK Guardian Poll Tracker, RealClearPolitics, 31 October 2020). You may now wish to evaluate the polls in the light of the outcome (Forsberg, 2020). For a useful account of the theory and practice of polling, see Moon (1999).

Fink, A. (1995). *How to sample in surveys.* Sage.

Fink offers a more general and accessible guide to sampling.

6

CREATING DATA: AN INTRODUCTION TO SURVEYS AND QUESTIONNAIRES

Chapter Overview

What are surveys?

Surveys are possibly the most maligned scientific instrument there is. Everyone thinks they can undertake surveys; they are often seen by the public as marketing scams, and they are often quite badly done. There are a lot of poor surveys around. Even amongst many quantitative researchers, design and implementation take second place to analysis. Everyone seems to want 'feedback', and we are bombarded with questionnaires. It's hardly surprising then that in recent years the number of people responding to government/academic surveys and political polling has declined. But well-designed surveys can provide excellent descriptive and explanatory data. Sometimes the importance of good survey and questionnaire design is overlooked in the desire to produce rigorous analyses. Yet however sophisticated our statistical analysis is, it is only as good as the data collection used to generate the data. We can think of surveys rather narrowly as collecting data on attributes, attitudes, behaviours and beliefs, but the techniques of the survey and the kind of data that can be collected are very much broader.

Several volumes in this series will refer to data from quite large-scale surveys, or administrative data. These data sets may hold data from many thousands, even hundreds of thousands, of people. They seem far removed from the humble survey being conducted in a shopping mall by a market researcher. Yet like Yorkshire Terriers and Great Danes, they share many characteristics (and sometimes faults). Take the biggest administrative data set of all in a country– the census (take your pick, USA, UK, France, New Zealand etc.). The census is so called because it covers the whole population of a country, not because of what it does methodologically. The census (in those countries that have one) gathers data on a wide range of characteristics through survey questions! Indeed, questions derived from censuses and used in other surveys are often deemed the 'gold standard', because the quality of data collection is assured through a number of quality control procedures (Dorling, 2007).[i]

But what of 'administrative data', that is collected by governments – births, deaths, employment/unemployment, GDP (gross domestic product) and so on? Indeed, these do not use survey questions, but the measures they do use are themselves both socially constructed and of varying **reliability** and **validity** (we'll come back to these). Crime statistics, for example, are often collected by police officers who must use their judgement as to whether something is a crime or what kind of crime it is.

Some of the best survey practice, in terms of design and data collection, comes in the very large surveys that may be, for example, panel studies or large cross-sectional

---

[i]See also, for example, www.ons.gov.uk/census/2011census/howourcensusworks/howwetookthe2011census/howweprocessedtheinformation/dataqualityassurance

national surveys (see Chapter 4). The quality of these is derived from the resources available to collect, code and analyse the data – resources not available to researchers conducting small-scale bespoke surveys.

Now you may plan to design your own survey and intend using secondary data from a large-scale survey or administrative resource. You may then think that what goes into data collection is not really relevant to you. But it is, because your analyses are derived originally from a series of questions and measures and will only be as good as these. So, for example, if you are interested in religious belief and you are using secondary data to conduct your research, it is best to know exactly how religious belief was measured through the questions asked and how the questions were asked. For example, did the survey ask about attendance at places of worship or did it ask about belief in a god or gods? Two quite different concepts. If a question is presented as a set of categories, for example, if age is only asked in age bands, then you potentially lose information as you cannot have information on particular years of age.

We can say that surveys (and to some extent administrative data) fall into two kinds. Those which collect data to answer a specific research question (see Chapter 2) and those which are there specifically as a resource for secondary analysis. Whilst these latter surveys are far from socially 'neutral' in the questions they ask – that is, the questions themselves will emerge from views on what might be the most useful and the important data to collect – they do not attempt to answer any specific question or questions. Secondary analysis is discussed in depth in Volume 5.

Types of data collection in surveys

The type of data collection used will depend on a number of things, but the two most important are resources (see Chapter 4) and the kind of data you want to collect. Data collection, in surveys, divides into two main kinds: self-completion and data collected through interviewers. There are hybrids of these too, such as the use of video, and a new form of data collection (technically in the second kind) is the use of avatars as interviewers (http://home.isr.umich.edu/sampler/testing-tomorrows-surveys-today-avatars-as-interviewers).

We now turn to the main types of data collection and their variants.

Face-to-face Interviews

This is possibly the most traditional and recognisable way in which surveys are conducted. One has the image of a market researcher with a clipboard. But face-to-face interviews can be of many different kinds, some very sophisticated.

The venue of interviews makes a difference. Interviews may be conducted in public places, in respondents' homes or workplace, and increasingly, people have started using video methods, often through Skype or Zoom. Public places, such as streets, are only suitable for very short interviews, because the respondents will have only just been recruited and most are going about their business with little time to participate in a lengthy interview.

Major studies, such as the UK panel study *Understanding Society* (www.understand ingsociety.ac.uk), often conduct interviews in respondents' homes (Understanding Society also uses online self-completion methods). These interviews can last for 2 hours or more, and several members of the household may be interviewed. Consequently, in these interviews, interviewers can help the respondent to provide an adequate response by prompting or probing particular aspects of respondents' lives in great depth and produce very rich data (Sykes & Collins, 1992).

At the opposite end of the spectrum, we have very short surveys conducted in public places which ask only a very few questions. An example of this is the UK *International Passenger Survey*, which conducts between 600,000 and 700,000 short interviews annually (www.ons.gov.uk/peoplepopulationandcommunity/leisureand-tourism/methodologies/internationalpassengersurveymethodology).

Face-to-face interviews allow both for probes, where the interviewer can attempt to elicit a more detailed answer from the respondent, and the use of open-ended questions, where the interviewer can record verbatim a response in the respondent's own words. Open-ended questions can be used in self-completion surveys, but they rely on the respondent writing their own answers.

In larger-scale surveys paper-based interview schedules have all but completely been made redundant through the use of computer-assisted personal interviews (CAPI). Interviewers use laptops with software that can 'customise' interviews. Depending on an answer given by a respondent, the software will route the interviewer to different next questions. This has been used in paper interview schedules for a very long time, but in CAPI there is less room for interviewer error, and the routing used can be very much more sophisticated.

So, what are the advantages and disadvantages of face-to-face interviews?

Box 6.1

Advantages and Disadvantages of Face-to-Face Interviews

Advantages

- Questions can be more complex.
- Depending on setting, interviews may be used to ask more questions than in self-completion questionnaires.

- Open-ended questions, probes and prompts can be used.
- The interviewer has control over who responds.
- The interviewer can build a relationship with the respondent that allows for the exploration of complex or sensitive issues. This is also useful in panel studies, where a good relationship over time between researchers and respondents is important.
- Visual aids, such as cards, images or video clips, can be used.
- Multiple household, or group interviews, can be conducted in the same time frame and place.

Disadvantages

- Interviewing skills. Interviewing is a skilled task and poor interviewing can lead to bias.
- Time limitations. Setting up and conducting interviews is resource intensive, both in time and the use of interviewers (who often must be paid).
- Interviewer effects. Interviewers may have an 'effect' on respondents. Age, sex, ethnicity, accent, attitude or appearance can make a difference to how respondents answer questions.
- Anonymity. In self-completion surveys, respondent anonymity can be achieved. In interviews, though the data may be anonymised, the interviewer is directly asking things of the respondent, and this may lead the respondent to withhold sensitive information.
- Social desirability. Almost the opposite, in that the respondent will be keen to please the interviewer and attempt to give answers that she or he thinks are correct or desirable.

Telephone interviewing

Telephone interviewing has also been around a long time, but with the advent of mobile phones its character and issues of access and sampling have changed. Traditional telephone interviews utilised 'lists', such as telephone directories, and were conducted via home-based telephones, with the interviewer using paper and pen questionnaires. A major issue then was that a sizeable proportion of the population did not have access to a telephone. This approach to telephone interviewing was described, as late as 1994, in a guide written by Roger Thomas and Susan Purdon (Thomas & Purdon, 1994). But things have changed rapidly since then; but having said this, some of the essential character, advantages and disadvantages, still hold. For a broad historical perspective on changes in survey research methodology, see Groves (2011).

Telephone interviewing allows many of the techniques of face-to-face interviews to be used, but the contact is wholly aural, with video interviews possibly occupying some kind of middle ground between face-to-face interviews and self-completion surveys. It is generally held that telephone interviews must be shorter than face-to-face interviews, and this is certainly the case when they are conducted using mobile phones.

Telephone interviews permit a more rapid access to respondents, without the need to travel, which makes them less resource intensive. Furthermore, face-to-face interviews usually require some form of clustering in sampling (see Chapter 5 and Volume 4), to cut down geographical dispersion (and therefore travelling for the interviewer), but telephone interviews do not.

Nowadays, telephone interviews employ more sophisticated technologies, such as random digit dialling, for sample selection (although this has been around for a while), and computer-assisted telephone interviewing (CATI), somewhat similar in its utility to CAPI. The challenge for telephone interviewing, however, is that home-based telephone access is actually less representative of populations than it was. Fewer people now have access to home-based phones, in Western countries, than for many decades. These are not necessarily older people or poorer people, who cannot afford phone access, but also include many young and often relatively affluent people. So, mobile phones are becoming the medium more commonly used, but this presents some technical and ethical problems. The first relates to things like signal strength and suitability of location for the respondent (noise, distractions etc.) and length of time the respondent can give to the interviewer, usually considered less than in traditional telephone interviews. The second is primarily about the safety of the respondent, who may be driving, or in another environment where answering a mobile phone may present dangers. Or it may be, because of things like roaming charges, that the respondent may incur costs. To some extent, these things can be overcome by recruitment through prior texts or other means of electronic communication.

If these kind of issues can be overcome, then the use of mobile phones in interviews does potentially open access to millions more respondents, particularly in developing countries, where mobile phones are very much more prevalent than fixed land-based ones. Furthermore, sampling through mobile numbers, linked to social media data, may prove to be a useful way of connecting individual information to anonymised large-scale data from Twitter feeds and so on.

Finally, however, in the past few years, the biggest enemy of telephone interviewing has become the ubiquitous telephone sales call, often disguised as a 'telephone interview', though again this is (at present) less of a problem with mobile phones.

Box 6.2

Advantages and Disadvantages of Telephone Interviewing

Advantages

- Faster contact with respondents, is less resource intensive and requires no travelling for interviewers.

- Larger samples remove the need for geographic clustering.
- Use of mobile phones can potentially reach new populations.
- Because contact is aural only, there can be fewer interviewer effects.

Disadvantages

- Making contact and securing an interview can be challenging, particularly since the growth of telesales.
- Fewer people have telephones at home, and this presents sampling problems.
- Mobile phone contact has technical and ethical issues.
- Questions must be simpler, and visual aids cannot be used.
- Rapport is more difficult without face-to-face contact.
- Response categories must be fewer, because the respondent cannot be expected to memorise complex or multiple possible responses.

Self-completion surveys

The commonest mode of surveying is self-completion. However, like telephone surveys the landscape of self-completion has changed dramatically in the past decade or so, with fewer and fewer 'paper' questionnaires being used. These will probably not disappear altogether, because paper questionnaires remain useful for short simple surveys conducted in public places. For example, train operators, in several countries, use paper onboard or railway station-based passenger questionnaires. However, increasingly, self-completion has moved online.

Before we talk about the specifics of particular modes of data collection, we will briefly mention some common characteristics of self-completion surveys. The main reason for using self-completion is scale and speed. Whatever resources one has to conduct face-to-face interviews, time is one resource that is always finite. Self-completion allows for a large number of people to be contacted quickly, either through electronic means, face to face (as in the above-mentioned transport surveys) or by post. However, because the respondent must complete the survey themselves, questions must be relatively simple, and open-ended questions may not provide the richness of data that face-to-face or telephone surveys will provide. On the other hand, because the respondent can see the questions, or other visual aids, there can be a little more complexity than in telephone surveys.

Also, contrary to popular belief, it is possible to ask sensitive questions in a self-completion format because there is no interviewer for the respondent to have to interact with and indeed no interviewer effects. As Anne Bowling (2005: 287) put it,

Self-administration of questionnaires can increase respondents' willingness to disclose sensitive information, compared with face-to-face or telephone interviews. The greater anonymity offered in postal survey, with its weak social presence, for example, has been reported to lead to high item response, and more accurate reporting on sensitive topics such as health and behaviour.

Possibly the biggest generic issue for self-completion is non-response or item non-response (the latter where the respondent does not answer a particular question or questions). Postal, email and internet surveys commonly achieve response rates of less than 20%, and moreover, non-response has been growing (Groves, 2006). This is particularly prevalent in the under 25 years age group and those in lower socio-economic groups. Item non-response (see Chapter 7) can be overcome to *some* extent through different forms of imputation, whereby data gathered elsewhere in the questionnaire is used to impute the missing answers. During the last 20 years, there has been a massive expansion in the development and practice of procedures to handle item non-response, and whilst the topic does not have a dedicated volume in this series, interested readers may like to consult Durrant (2005) for an appreciation of the variety of approaches. In some online surveys the respondent is not permitted to move on to the next question if they do not answer the prior one. This strategy has its dangers, and we do not advocate it, because there is every possibility the respondent will abandon the survey at this point, and item non-response becomes respondent non-response! Literacy problems can be an issue, and there is no control over who completes the questionnaire. A final last generic issue for each mode of data collection is that self-completion questionnaires must be short, and a great deal of thought must go into question order and category order in possible responses. We will come back to that below.

Paper questionnaires are much less flexible than electronic ones. The skips or routing to later questions, depending on prior answers, must be very simple. Data gathered from them has to be manually entered into a database or analysis application. A respondent, given a paper questionnaire, can look at the whole questionnaire, and this may determine how or whether they complete it.

Electronic questionnaires can come in many different types. They may be accessed through embedded URLs, attached to emails, or use a platform used by particular communities such as Facebook. Increasingly they are being developed for smartphone use. The biggest issue is that of sampling (see Chapter 5). In short, a self-selection approach, whereby a request to complete a questionnaire is made available to large numbers of people (e.g. through Facebook), will almost certainly introduce selection bias and produce a skewed sample. The first can be addressed to some extent through the use of psychometrics in the design of the questions, though a skill beyond most researchers. The second can be addressed to some extent through quota sampling and 'weighting' responses, where groups are under-represented.

Online surveys (also described as web or internet surveys), nevertheless, have huge and growing advantages (Tourangeau et al., 2013). There are simple but effective design applications such as Google Forms,[ii] SurveyMonkey[iii] or Qualtrics.[iv] The first two are free to use but somewhat less versatile than the third, which for most purposes requires a licence. In Qualtrics, questions can be sequenced and made bespoke to particular respondents, in much the same way as in CAPI or CATI, visuals or audio can be embedded and meta-data such as overall completion time, or question completion time, be obtained. Data can be automatically imported into databases or analysis packages, permitting ongoing production of frequencies and so on. But, perhaps, the greatest attraction is the ability to reach vast numbers of people very quickly. But, this said, assuming that one does not wish to allow self-selection, getting access to sampling frames (say within universities, companies or government) can be difficult because of confidentiality issues. In wider public surveys, sampling frames are even harder to find. Traditional lists, such as voter lists, postcodes and so on, cannot be linked to electronic addresses.

Box 6.3

Advantages and Disadvantages of Self-Completion Surveys

Advantages

- Relatively quick access to large numbers of respondents, so larger samples
- Less resource-intensive
- New software permits relatively complex questionnaires that do not appear complex to respondents
- Online questionnaires can easily embed audio or visual content
- No geographical limits and therefore no need for clustering
- Can permit the asking of sensitive questions
- Can be accessed on mobile devices
- No interviewer effects

Disadvantages

- Non-response and item non-response more likely
- Limits on probing and what data can be obtained through open-ended questions
- Online surveys have particular sampling problems
- Paper questionnaires must be very simple
- No researcher control over who completes the survey
- Issues of access for those with poor literacy

We turn now to questionnaire design.

[ii]Google Forms: www.google.co.uk/forms/about
[iii]SurveyMonkey: www.surveymonkey.co.uk
[iv]Qualtrics: www.qualtrics.com

Types of measurement in surveys

Before beginning to design a questionnaire we have to think about what it is we are trying to measure, and this will impact on the kinds of questions used and the measurements they produce. So, throughout the question writing process, we need to consider the types of measurement that will ensue. What we have called types of measurement is often referred to as 'levels of measurement', but briefly we use the word *type* to indicate that particular questions will yield types of answers that have to be analysed in quite different ways and the relationships between types of measurement, within one survey, will set limits on the type of statistic that can be used (see other volumes in this series, but particularly Volumes 3 and 8). Thus, there are different mathematical and logical relations behind these measurement types; thus, how one asks a question and the categories of answers available will make important differences to subsequent analyses.

That they are often called levels of measurement is because they ascend from (mathematically) the simplest level of nominal measurement to the mathematically more sophisticated ratio or metric measurement. They are then as follows:

Nominal: Sometimes this level is called categorical, for it simply measures categories without any ranking at all. Ethnicity, for example, might be measured through several named categories plus an 'other' category, but being a member of one ethnic group does not imply any mathematical value in relation to another but simply a different category.

Ordinal: There remains a level of ranking here, but the differences between the ranks need not be equal. We may wish to measure level of educational achievement by asking the respondent to specify level of qualification attained. A master's degree is not twice the value of a bachelor's degree, for example.

Interval: Interval-level measurement is often used to measure characteristics of the physical world, such as temperature measured as Celsius or Fahrenheit. Interval data have no true zero, though the points on the scale must be equidistant – thus, the 'intervals'. Measurements, such as temperature, are arbitrary. Interval-level measurement is relatively uncommon in social science.

Ratio/metric: Ratio scales are scales which begin from a true zero but in which adjoining values are the same distance apart. Income, for example, can begin from zero dollars or euros and so on and rise to whatever you wish to measure. Scores on a ratio scale may be multiplied and divided, but those on an interval scale can only be added and subtracted.

Questionnaire design: some preliminaries

Before thinking about survey questions, there are some questions that you must ask yourself. First, who are you asking – that is, what is your target population? This will make a difference to what you ask and how you ask it. For example, if you are interested in exploring youth issues, you will need to ask different questions of young people than if you were asking older people their views of young people. Crucially, what is the mode of data collection? Face-to-face interviews, self-completion either online or paper questions, telephone interviews and so on.

Most questionnaires these days use some form of template, whether they are for online use or as interview schedules. In the first case, SurveyMonkey has both a good website to help you and a number of pre-existing templates you can use for your questionnaire (www.surveymonkey.com/mp/how-to-create-surveys). Administered questionnaires must be designed for ease of use and to avoid error by the interviewer. If this is done through CAPI or CATI, then there should be a number of screens that are not too busy that the interviewer works through. Likewise, paper questionnaires should not be busy and filters/routings clear for the interviewer.

There are also some generic rules for all types of self-completion questionnaire. Questions should be phrased simply and clearly, and initial questions should not 'put the respondent off'. Particularly, you should not open with sensitive or difficult questions. Repetitive ways of asking questions should be avoided, and especially, one should avoid 'grids' that respondents must complete. What should be avoided is that respondents should not be just going through the motions, or answering with what they think is the 'right answer' (called satisficing; see Krosnick et al., 1996). For an illustration of the effect of changing modes of data collection for a comparison of self-completion and face-to-face interviewing, see Cannell and Fowler (1963).

Asking questions

What you ask and how you ask it depends on context. A survey, whether self-completion or through interviews, is a social act, requiring not simply the professional skills of the researcher but also a great deal of tacit knowledge on the part of the respondent. To participate in a survey requires a lot of tacit cultural knowledge that in Western cultures are taken for granted. The researcher needs to be sensitive to other factors such as age or disability, or when a self-completion questionnaire (or any questionnaire for that matter) would be inappropriate. Even amongst those quite capable of participating in a survey, it is important to be sure that they have sufficient knowledge to be able to answer the questions. A good survey will have questions appropriate to the target population's ability to answer and will have questions that a respondent will want to answer. Certain kinds of questions will evoke particular responses that you do not want, or non-response, or you may bore the respondent to non-completion!

Questionnaires are not just questions! They will contain instructions to the respondent, or interviewer; they will contain 'filters' to take some respondents on different routes to others. In CAPI and CATI, this is performed by the software, though interview schedules will often contain things that are to be read out by the interviewer or visual aids to be used, such as showcards. In online, self-completion surveys, there may be embedded materials, such as videos or vignettes. The format of all types of survey may be very 'closed', providing a limited number of responses to be chosen, or the respondent may be encouraged to respond in their own words in 'open' questions. Again, in online questionnaires, respondents can manipulate words or icons on the screen to produce preferences or rankings.

Most questionnaires will contain different kinds of questions. Firstly, factual questions about *attributes*, such as the following:

How many bedrooms do you have in your house or apartment?

They may be about *attitudes*, such as the following:

Do you think that cars with high exhaust emissions should be subject to higher taxes?

They may be about *beliefs*, such as the following:

Do you believe in the existence of UFOs (unidentified flying objects)?

Or they may be about *behaviour*, such as the following:

Which of the following countries have you visited in the last 5 years?

Beliefs and attitudes are not always easily separated. For example, it is possible to use the language of beliefs to describe political attitudes, say a 'belief in socialism', and attitude scales often measure how strongly someone believes something to be the case. It is possible, therefore, to use such language interchangeably about questions of both knowledge and opinion. In either case, we can hold opinions or our certainty in knowing particular things with different intensities (Oppenheim, 1992, p. 176). Political opinion will often be stronger than an opinion about the merits of one kind of food over another, and depending on levels of certainty, questions of knowledge can shade into attributes. For example, a question such as the following:

What do you believe to be the average waiting time to see your doctor?

The doctor is likely to know this, but members of the public could answer with some actual knowledge, or simply a guess. For most, it would be the latter.

Many ask questions about beliefs and attitudes through statements with which the respondent is asked to express agreement/disagreement (we will return to this below).

When considering the content of questionnaire, it is worth remembering that others have been there before, and often there are well-tested questions that can be used in a variety of contexts. The researcher can benefit from the development of questions designed by others, but also a standardisation of certain questions permits comparison between studies. In the last few years a number of question 'banks' have been established, often containing well-tested questions from large government surveys. For example, the UK Data Service has a 'bank' of questions and variables that can be searched (https://discover.ukdataservice.ac.uk/variables). Another related development has been the recognition of the importance of harmonising data so that routine questions are standardised across repeat surveys (see Cohort and Longitudinal Studies Enhancement Resources www.closer.ac.uk).

Most surveys will also contain 'face sheet information', sometimes called 'classifying' or 'personal' data (Oppenheim, 1992, p. 109) and in the USA 'demographic data'. This is background information on the attributes of respondents that allows comparison both across the survey and between surveys on the variables operationalised from the research question. Face sheet variables usually include sex, age, ethnicity and social class. In Western societies, these are key defining variables and often can explain important differences in attitudes and attributes. There are differing views on where face sheet information should be placed. If used at the beginning of a survey, a battery of such questions may seem irrelevant or intrusive to the respondent, and mostly it is better to place them at the end of the questionnaire. But if you are using quota sampling (see Chapter 5) in face-to-face interviewing, the researcher needs to ask at least some of these questions to establish whether the respondent is 'in scope' for the sample.

Designing questions and designing surveys

How questions and surveys are designed depends a lot on whether they are self-completion (then online or paper) or whether they are interviews (face-to-face or telephone). However, there are some generic principles. We will approach this section through generic principles (because in an introductory book such as this space is limited).

In phrasing our questions, we are seeking a 'stimulus equivalence' (Oppenheim, 1992, p. 121), between the question and the response and between respondents. That is, when we ask respondent A a question she understands what we understand by it. Likewise respondents B, C, D and so on also understand what we understand by it. However, with few exceptions there is no necessary or direct correspondence between asking and finding out. In everyday conversations, we have the opportunity to clarify meaning and correct misunderstanding through subsidiary questions or statements. In questionnaires, we cannot establish this kind of folk validity, because the need for reliability (we will come to this below) requires us to ask the same question of each respondent in the same way. Elucidation or clarification is not usually permissible. Moreover, just because someone answered your question it doesn't mean that they understood it in the same way as someone else did, or that their answer meant the same thing.

Types of question

As we said above, questions can be approximately divided into those that ask about facts, behaviour, attitudes and beliefs. A good starting strategy is to see which of the 'rough' questions fall into each of these categories and then consider the best ways of asking them.

Categorical questions

The commonest and simplest of questions are categorical. There may be yes or no answers or just categories in which the respondent must choose only one. These correspond to the nominal level of measurement described above. For example, we might ask students a question as shown in Figure 6.1.

Which of the following best describes the kind of place you live in?	
House	☐
Apartment/flat	☐
University campus accommodation	☐
Other (please specify)	☐

Figure 6.1 Categorical questions

They may be categorical questions, but the respondent may choose more than one category. For example, see Figure 6.2:

Although each of these examples is a factual question, the same format can be used for behaviour, attitudes or beliefs. In the example in Figure 6.2, we may have asked, 'Which of the following vegetables do you never eat and provide a list?'

Which of the following vegetables, fresh or frozen, have you eaten at least once in the past week? Please select all that you have eaten.

Peas	☐
Cabbage	☐
Carrots	☐
Cauliflower	☐
Green beans	☐
Sweet corn	☐
Swede/turnip	☐

Figure 6.2 Categorical questions – more than one category

Ordered categories

Quite often we want respondents to place things in some kind of order, perhaps of preference. Such responses are categories, but they are ordered categories, though we do not quantify the difference between categories. These correspond to ordinal-level measurement. We may ask, as in Figure 6.3, for the respondent to estimate the likelihood of Australia winning the Ashes in cricket. We cannot assume that, in their answer to this question, respondents who answered 'very high' are saying that they think Australia is five times more likely to win the Ashes than someone who answered 'very low', but nevertheless we must suppose that the respondent is providing a personal estimate of the probability of victory and that there is a ranking, which corresponds to an ordinal-level of measurement.

How do you rate the chances of Australia winning the Ashes this year?

Very high	☐
High	☐
Moderate	☐
Low	☐
Very low	☐
Not sure	☐

Figure 6.3 Ordered categories

Semantic differential scales

Attitude scales use a series of questions, which are designed to measure the strength of attitudes and beliefs. There are many different kinds of scales, but here we describe two of the commonest.

In the first of these, semantic differential scales, respondents are asked to locate their attitudes on a scale ranging between opposite positions on a particular issue, described by bipolar attitudes or phrases. Some things, such as income, height, distance and so on, fall naturally into this type, but other things, especially to do with attitudes or beliefs, do not. They need a little bit of help, and semantic differential scales provide such help.

For example, the question in Figure 6.3 could have been asked like this:

I'd like to ask you about your views on the chances of Australia winning the Ashes this year. On a scale of 1 to 10, where 10 is very likely for them to win this year and 1 is very unlikely, what do you think the likelihood is?

Here the language of measurement is very much more explicit and allows us to treat the response as if it had the same mathematical properties as (say) distance, or height.

One question can also be used to explore a number of dimensions using opposites, as shown in Figure 6.4. (*Note:* Quite a few more dimensions would be needed in this particular example.)

How would you evaluate your module in research methods?		
Easy	1 2 3 4 5 6 7 8 9	Difficult
Detailed	1 2 3 4 5 6 7 8 9	Superficial
Too much statistics	1 2 3 4 5 6 7 8 9	Not enough statistics
Too much ethnography	1 2 3 4 5 6 7 8 9	Not enough ethnography

Figure 6.4   Semantic differential scales

A further word of caution about what we are measuring. When we measure the distance in kilometres between A and B, unless we were mistaken, each of us would come up independently with the same answer. If we ask Jane and Joe to assess their chances of promotion at work, for example, Jane may be a pessimist and Joe an optimist in relation to their 'real' chances, but they both answer 6. We now turn to the second kind of scale in common use, the Likert scale.

Likert scales

If single questions are asking about factual things, provided the respondent understands the question and has the information to answer it, then these questions are usually quite reliable, but single questions about attitudes, beliefs and behaviour often are not. Now, properly asked there is nothing wrong with these, but in most surveys that measure such things, some kind of **scaling** is used to ask a 'battery' of questions. Likert scales, which also can measure beliefs, can consist of anything between 6 and 30 items, though 30 items would certainly test the endurance of most respondents!

As Oppenheim (1992, p. 187) warns us, these are overt measuring instruments, and we should not expect too much of them – that is, they may only approximate to respondents' views. Nevertheless, in recent years, 'scaling' has become quite sophisticated, but given the introductory level of this book, heed should be paid to Oppenheim's warning of limitations.

Likert scales use a matrix to ask a number of attitudinal questions at the same time. One advantage of this is that in analysis respondents can be allocated an overall 'score' for adherence toward a particular attitude. The scale will usually consist of a number of statements the respondent is asked to agree or disagree with. These statements should be measuring different dimensions of the same topic.

Figure 6.5 shows a simple example – in this case from a face-to-face interview – but Likert scales are commonly used in a self-completion format.

I'd like to read out some things people have said about their current employment. Would you please say whether you strongly agree, agree, disagree or strongly disagree with each?				
	Strongly Agree	Agree	Disagree	Strongly Disagree
I feel valued by my employer	☐	☐	☐	☐
My career prospects are good	☐	☐	☐	☐
I am constantly under pressure	☐	☐	☐	☐
I see no future for me in this job	☐	☐	☐	☐
I have an opportunity to use my skills	☐	☐	☐	☐
My employer doesn't listen to employees	☐	☐	☐	☐
My work–life balance is good	☐	☐	☐	☐

Figure 6.5   Likert scales

Notice that the statements can be either positive or negative and that these are mixed together. A disadvantage of this is that in self-completion questionnaire, with a large number of positive and negative statements, a respondent may accidentally treat a positive as a negative and vice versa. However, the advantages probably outweigh the disadvantages, not just in terms of space saved but also as a validity check. How is this done? Well, in a large number of items, a positive and a negative version of the same measure may be interspersed. If, for example, a respondent strongly agreed with both the first and the sixth statement in Figure 6.5, then we would have cause to worry about the validity of the measure.

However, such contradiction is not uncommon and may be the result of layout, wording or a problem with the level of knowledge of the respondent (see Oppenheim,

1992, p. 147). For this reason alone, piloting of the questionnaire and the pretesting of the items in it are important.

Notice that in Figure 6.5 the respondents are asked about levels of agreement/disagreement, but this could be different, and with a slight rewording of the statements, we could ask the following:

> How satisfied are you with the following aspects of your job? Very satisfied, satisfied, neither satisfied nor dissatisfied.

In this example, there are only a few dimensions, but scales may often contain more, or several scales are used (see Linacre, 2002).

Finally, the question of a 'neutral' middle category is a rather vexed issue. Sometimes, as in the above example, a category of 'neither satisfied nor dissatisfied' is in itself a useful one, because it is being made to 'do some work', but often it can function as an opt-out for respondents.

How bad questions lead to missing or poor data

We began this chapter by noting the existence of bad surveys. These can be bad for a number of reasons, such as poor sampling, non-response and commonly poor question wording or construction. This is not restricted to amateur surveys. For example, the 2017 version of a UK rail passenger survey asked passengers to state how many minutes late their completed journey was, *during* their journey!

Question wording is something of an art, though its quality is made scientific through rigorous pretesting. Though it should be added that a form of words that constitutes a bad question in one context may work well in another. What follows is not definitive but should be seen as a guide to getting the questions right. A good way to get a feel for what is right is to consider what can go wrong.

Ambiguity

This can occur in a number of ways. A common error is to ask two or more things in the same question, what are called 'double-barrelled questions'. For example,

> Are you satisfied with your job and pay? Yes/No.

Is the respondent answering yes to being satisfied with her job, her pay or both?

Negatives are another source of ambiguity. For example,

> Do you not agree with not reviewing your pay? Agree/Disagree

Irrelevancy

The following is an example of making people answer irrelevant questions, such as asking someone who is unemployed,

How much do you earn?

Frame of reference

The frame of reference, to do with time or amount of something, might also be ambiguous. For example,

Have you been doing this job for a long time? Yes/No

or

How much do you earn?

Necessary knowledge

Surveys are often about quite specialist topics, but respondents may not have the necessary knowledge to answer a direct question. For example, the answer to the question

Do you agree with the government's long-term plans to boost national productivity?

will depend on whether the person knows what is meant by productivity and specifically what the government means by it and what its plans are. If you were an economist, it might be a legitimate topic, but even then, the question would need to be broken down into specifics.

These are brief examples of bad questions, and the problems such questions cause can be avoided or mitigated through a strategy of using tried and tested questions, perhaps using, as suggested above, a question bank or questions from reputable surveys and through a thorough pretesting and piloting of the questions and questionnaire. If you are conducting secondary analysis, it is important to look at the original questionnaire to see how the question was asked and where in the questionnaire it was asked.

Reliability and validity

A well-designed questionnaire maximises reliability and validity. The first refers to how reliable the 'instrument' or question is, and poor reliability produces more 'random error' in a survey (Litwin, 1995); the second refers to how valid, as a measurement, it is, and poor validity results from measurement error.

Reliability can be summarised as the consistency or stability of a measure, test or observation from one use to the next. When repeated measurements of the same thing give highly similar results, the measurement instrument is said to be reliable. For example, if your watch or clock is gaining or losing, or your bathroom scales give quite different readings each time you use them, then they are unreliable.

When a survey is conducted, on repeated occasions, it is important that any differences in response between people, or over time if asked of the same person, are the result of different circumstances and not something to do with the survey, questions, scales and so on within it.

Most national surveys will check back for consistency of response (see the link above to the UK Office for National Statistics). This can be done by asking a person at time t_1 a series of questions about themselves and repeating this at time t_2 (see de Vaus, 2014, p. 54) or comparing the respondent's answers on some objective measure.

The UK censuses ask questions about the number of rooms a household has for its own use (see https://blog.ons.gov.uk/2017/06/28/an-alternative-approach-to-estimating-number-of-rooms-and-bedrooms/).

Although guidance is provided on what counts as a 'room', the responses given are subject to high levels of misclassification. The reliability of the measure is established by an interviewer returning to a sample of households and asking a series of detailed questions about the accommodation, the answers to which are checked against the original census return for the household.

How does unreliability arise? In the previous example, it arose from respondents differently classifying a room. The fault therefore lies with the question, but it should be said this is a hard thing to measure. Unreliability frequently does arise from respondents understanding the question differently or not being in a position to answer the question (see the examples above), but in face-to-face interviews it can also arise from interviewer effects, such as the age, sex, dress or ethnic background of the interviewer, vis-à-vis the respondent. Reliability can be improved in a number of ways. In face-to-face interviews through the training of interviewers and matching them to the appropriate populations and in all cases through consistency checks of data entry, but mostly through the thorough testing of the questionnaire and items within it.

A survey can be reliable without being valid. Consistency of response may be obtained, but that consistency may be due to consistent misinterpretation by the respondent, or the particular question or scale may not be measuring what it is supposed to be measuring. A watch that is consistently 5 minutes fast is reliable but not a valid measure of time!

The validity of a survey, whether it is measuring what it is supposed to measure, is an important issue, and there are different forms of validity (see Litwin, 1995). Perhaps the most important is construct validity. *Construct validity* refers to the extent to which variables accurately measure the constructs of interest. For example, health and illness can be measured in different ways, but particular measures in isolation will not necessarily validly measure the health of a respondent. It is quite legitimate to ask a question, or questions, about how a respondent feels, but this is subjective and two people, with say a similar health problem, may answer differently. In addition, we could ask them about hospital visits, doctors' visits over time or whether they had suffered, or were suffering from, particular illnesses. But these latter questions would not tell us how the person felt!

A related form of construct validity is referred to as *criterion validity*, which has an important role to play as a *screening* instrument. Its application depends upon what the researcher holds to be an external arbiter of true state. For example, the results of the application of a self-completion questionnaire (the General Health Questionnaire) to assess a respondent's psychiatric state were contrasted to a professional psychiatrist evaluation during a re-interview (Tarnopolsky et al., 1979) in the context of a community survey. The questionnaire was reported to have misclassified 25% of the respondents.

Arguably, one will never achieve perfect construct validity, but prior research to develop the categories can improve it (see Ahmad, 1999, for a discussion of this). As Mark Litwin (1995) observes, 'Construct validity is the most valuable yet most difficult way of assessing a survey instrument [and] . . . is often determined only after years of experience with a survey instrument' (p. 43). Construct validity is closely related to content validity, the latter referring to whether the survey instrument captures all of the important dimensions of the thing being measured, as opposed to the specific measure.

Descending the ladder of abstraction

Finally, by way of a recap, we conclude with the issue of *operationalisation*. Operationalisation begins in the abstract, in the form of a theory that we wish to test. It then needs to be turned into research questions that become testable hypotheses and then questions that are capable of being answered by a population, and that population is then capable of being researched through a survey or an experiment. Assuming we choose a survey, what is its mode of implementation – face-to-face interview, self-completion and so on? Then, what is it that is to be measured and how? How are these turned into concepts? This is where operationalisation actually takes place.

For example, in a study of the academic achievements of 'poor' school children, 'poor' could be operationalised as eligibility for school meals (Hobbs & Vignoles, 2010).

Finally, the concepts, such as eligibility for school meals, must be turned into questions that measure this. The whole process is often referred to as descending the ladder of abstraction. Each stage of the process, from theory conceptualisation right down to measurement through the question, will shape the data we have to analyse, and its quality.

Piloting and pretesting

Pretesting and piloting are the same concept, but the former usually refers to the testing of the whole instrument, in the field, whereas the latter refers to the testing of particular items. Often textbooks will index these things under 'piloting' (de Vaus, 2014; Litwin, 2003). For shorthand, we will use the term *piloting*.

Piloting is essential to the development of a good questionnaire. Even the most experienced survey researchers will uncover error, or discover better ways of administering the questionnaire, asking the questions or developing categories. The extent to which piloting can be done is, inevitably, a resource issue. Major national surveys will be rigorously piloted for months, but this will have to be scaled back for small-scale surveys.

David de Vaus (2014, p. 99) lists three stages of piloting:

1   *Question development:* Questions may be original to your questionnaire, or they may have been used in other surveys. In the second case, they may well have been tested, but the context in which you are using them (different questionnaire, possibly a different population) still means that they need to be tested. The questions need to be tested on people who closely resemble the population. They are told that they are helping to develop the questions in a pretest of a questionnaire, they are asked to answer the questions and then they themselves are asked questions about the questions, such as how did they understand the question; when they gave their answer, would they have had additional/other categories and would they have worded the question differently. When this is done in great depth, cognitive interviewing techniques might be used. They are particularly used in market research (see www.quirks.com/articles/how-cognitive-interviewing-can-improve-your-questionnaire-design for a further description).

2   *Questionnaire development:* Though individual questions can be improved through testing, when they are put together in a questionnaire, this may change the way respondents answer and may entail item non-response, so the next phase is to pilot the questionnaire with the pretested questions, the filters, the showcards and so forth, on a group of people who would likely have been in your sample. Usually, people are not told that they are part of a pilot. In Qualtrics, it is possible to collect data on the length of response to a question, or the questionnaire itself. Data from

pilot studies should not be included in your final sample data, because almost certainly you will have made changes.

3   *Polishing pilot test:* This is simply carrying out the changes from phases 1 and 2 into the final questionnaire. In very large-scale surveys, a further testing of the final instrument might be undertaken.

Conclusion

Although many of the volumes in this Kit are rightly concerned with analysis, the quality of survey design and questionnaire design is a prior condition to the quality of analyses. This chapter has been written to provide some rudimentary guidance on how one might go about designing a survey and questionnaire and the choices that need to be made. But, equally, if you are using secondary data, you should also review how these things were done. Additionally, you should review the sampling strategy and quality, but this is discussed in Chapter 5 and Volume 4. We would stress that we have not attempted to provide a comprehensive guide to design here and we would strongly recommend you consult the volumes in *The Survey Kit*, which is also published by Sage (see Further Reading) (https://uk.sagepub.com/en-gb/eur/the-survey-kit/book225666) or a classic text such as Oppenheim (1992).

Chapter Summary

- Your analyses of quantitative data will only be as good as the data collected. Most quantitative data comes from surveys, and this chapter is a brief introduction to surveys, explaining what they are, modes of data collection, some key issues in the design of questionnaires and some examples of bad questions!
- The chapter also introduces attitude scales and the important matter of validity and reliability.

Further Reading

We have not attempted to provide a comprehensive guide to design here, and we would strongly recommend you consult the volumes in the *SAGE Quantitative Kit* or a classic text such as the following:

Oppenheim, A. (1992). *Questionnaire design, interviewing and attitude measurement.* Pinter.

The principles of questionnaire and scale design in Oppenheim's book are timeless.

Czaja, R., Blair, J., & Blair, E. (2013). *Designing surveys: A guide to decision and process* (3rd ed.). Sage.

Czaja et al.'s book contextualises principles of questionnaire and scale design in newer forms of data collection, particularly in online research.

7

SECONDARY ANALYSIS AND DATA MANIPULATION

Chapter Overview

Introduction

Increasingly researchers are turning to conducting secondary analysis of existing data. This is sometimes referred to as archival analysis. Secondary analysis can refer to further analyses of any data, qualitative or quantitative, and data sets with many thousand cases to those with a few hundred or less. Indeed, in the UK, Essex University has for several decades been archiving a huge range of data sets, in all areas of social research, some excellent, some not so good. These are readily available to researchers to reanalyse at the UK Data Archive (http://data-archive.ac.uk). In recent years, the UK Data Service (www.ukdataservice.ac.uk) has been a portal for several large-scale secondary administrative data sources, available to researchers.

So why use **secondary data**? Not all secondary data are the same! A survey of a few hundred people, using a short questionnaire, will not provide much material for further analyses. Though, note, you may instead want to replicate a whole survey, or just some of the questions from such a survey, to provide comparative data between populations, or over time. For example, several studies, in the UK, of student understandings and perceptions of quantitative methods have used similar sets of questions, which permit both comparison and, in this case, further evidence to support shared research hypotheses (see e.g. Williams et al., 2017).

The secondary analysis of large data sets provides some significant advantages for researchers. These data sets are often the result of government surveys or censuses, or are conducted by universities or independent research centres, and they may well have gathered responses from several thousand people. Some of these surveys are 'panel' studies, and researchers return to the same respondents periodically, allowing a 'longitudinal' linkage of data so that people's lives, attitudes and beliefs can be followed through time. A good example of a panel study is *Understanding Society* (www.understandingsociety.ac.uk). Understanding Society is the largest panel study in the world. Over time, around 40,000 households have taken part, and their data leads to research, which informs policy in the UK. All the households in the study are visited by an interviewer or complete an online survey once a year. The questions asked cover a wide range of topics, for example, family life, education, employment, finance, health and well-being. Some questions are asked every year, whilst others are asked occasionally.

So the first advantage, of these kinds of studies, is the sheer number of cases, far more than a researcher would usually have the resources to gather data from. Crucially, such large numbers facilitate more complex, more interesting and more robust analyses. Analyses are more likely to be statistically significant (see Volumes 3 and 5) – that is, the finding is larger or smaller than would be expected by chance alone. A second advantage is data quality. Large-scale surveys are usually well resourced, which means that the questionnaires are rigorously tested and piloted before being used. In those surveys using face-to-face interviews, the interviewers will be trained professionals. There will often be 'back checking' (a sample of re-interviews typically carried out by supervisors or more experienced colleagues) of their interviews to ensure their quality. Data entry – that is, putting the response into a database, or analysis application, such as IBM® SPSS® Statistics Software ('SPSS') solely, will be checked and the data subsequently 'cleaned' to remove errors (see e.g. https://elit-edatascience.com/data-cleaning).

Using secondary data is a huge saving of resources for the researcher. They will have the data available, almost immediately, without need to collect it, thus saving time and money.

Finally, data can be recoded, and new variables can be created. For example, in the first instance, if the ages of all respondents are recorded in the database, then they can be recoded into the age bands appropriate to the current research. New variables can be created. For example, one of us wanted to create a new census variable that captured all types of household structure in order to measure the kind and number of people moving into, or out of, single-person households. Variables, such as the number of people, their sex and their relationship to each other, were measured and could be combined into a new composite variable called 'household structure' (Williams & Dale, 1991).

The above advantages may make you think 'why bother doing primary research'? Indeed, in many instances, this is a fair point to make – the advantages of the available data hugely outweigh the disadvantages. But there are some of the latter, and they are important. The first and obvious disadvantage is that the survey did not collect data that can adequately operationalise the variables that are of interest. For example, if you are interested in the relationship between education and later income, and data on income is not collected, then the data you have cannot properly answer the question. As we noted earlier, sometimes proxies can be used, but only for some variables. A rule of thumb would be that in a three-variable analysis only one proxy should be used.

A second important disadvantage is that although data quality is likely to be better in a large well-resourced study than that achieved with a much smaller resource, any errors or deficiencies in data collection are irretrievable and those of data entry and coding unlikely to be corrected. The main reason for this is that often you cannot know and indeed no one knows where the errors occurred.

There is a whole new area of secondary analyses that is growing rapidly in utility and popularity, described by three overlapping terms: (1) new social media data, (2) big data and (3) data mining. The first of these is 'naturally occurring data' from the internet and may include tweets, Facebook data, web page 'scraping' and so on.

Huge amounts are generated every second, and a whole new battery of techniques has been developed to analyse these data. Big data is more an umbrella term and may include the former, but it also includes things like transactional data from shopping preferences, population movement and so on. See, for example, a number of papers exploring these issues in the *International Journal of Social Research Methodology*, Volume 16, Issue 3, 2013. Finally, data mining is a new (well, fairly new) technique that searches for significant patterns in big data, rather than the more traditional variable-centred approach. These data, and approaches to analysis, offer new opportunities of massive analysis power that can often detect and predict ways of thinking and behaving invisible to more traditional methods (see Stephens and Sukumar, 2006). Indeed, they are able to successfully capture mathematical complexity in what would otherwise appear to be wholly stochastic behaviour.

Longitudinal data

Many of the very large national data sets, of the kind mentioned above, employ longitudinal designs (see Chapter 4). Indeed, it is in longitudinal studies that secondary analysis really comes into its own. In this chapter, our focus is on secondary longitudinal analyses, though some of the things we describe in the current chapter are relevant to the manipulation and analysis of primary data you may have collected yourself.

However, in order to take best advantage of the methods and techniques encountered in the other volumes in this *SAGE Quantitative Research Kit*, relatively large data sets are needed and mostly the methods and techniques described rely on secondary data. In order to demonstrate these methods and techniques, the remainder of this chapter is centred on a case study which draws upon a secondary longitudinal data source known as the National Child Development Study (NCDS): a sample of all those born in 1 week, in the UK, in March 1958 and followed throughout their lives. Our case study focuses upon the cohort members when they were aged 50 years.

Even though you are analysing secondary data, your study will still need ethical approval and should meet all relevant ethical standards (see Chapter 8 in this volume). Ethical approval is important, but with secondary surveys like NCDS, it's fairly straightforward, since all of the individuals are anonymised, and the data set contains no information about residential addresses.

Longitudinal data sets are rich in information about the life course. Although we inherit the topics and the content of the questions, it is important to familiarise oneself with the exact wording of the questions and how each longitudinal record has been constructed.

A major disadvantage with longitudinal data is, of course, that it is subject to attrition, as we will inevitably lose cohort members to the study over time. Attrition occurs when a person drops out of the study at a particular stage of data collection. In the administration of NCDS, there have been nine sweeps or waves of data collection, and there has been a steady loss to follow-up of around half of the original sample. In a minority of instances, people actually miss a sweep and return to the study at a later stage. A statistical advantage of having longitudinal data is that if someone drops out after the initial stage of data collection, we will have at least some (partial) information about them. This can be helpful if we want to impute or fill in missing data. We will say more about attrition in NCDS in Section 'Missing Data'.

When deciding to access a secondary data source, it is important to spend time finding out about these issues, just as you would invest time and effort in developing your own questionnaire for primary data collection. Our intention is to provide you with a method of going about your analysis, with plenty of signposting for the detail that follows in Volumes 2 (*Exploratory and Descriptive Statistics*) and 5 (*Archival and Secondary Data*). We will illustrate all analysis using SPSS software.

Consolidating your research questions

Under primary survey data collection, your survey questionnaire will operationalise your research questions. In contrast, when accessing a secondary data source, the available data will not necessarily embody or match your specific quest for answers to your research. That may well imply that you have to compromise or modify your research questions to fit whatever the data collected in the original study allow.

One strategic option would be to have a fairly general overarching research question which enables you to explore the influences of key phenomena without being too specific at the outset (see Chapter 2). But of course, whatever you decide upon, there is no avoiding the need to have a good grasp of the literature concerning previous studies in the topic area and perhaps studies which have used a similar methodological strategy or even the same data set (see Chapter 3). Your secondary analysis and research questions cannot be divorced from what has gone before: you must ensure you are not simply trying to prove what someone else has already shown, and you need an awareness of how your findings will impact on a changing policy landscape.

In our case study, we will explore the legacy which childhood leaves for adult well-being and cognitive functioning amongst UK adults entering the 'third age' (Laslett, 1989; Rowland, 2012). Policymakers have recently turned their attention from measures like 'gross domestic product' per head of population to measures such as happiness and well-being (Layard, 2006; Tennant et al., 2007; Wiggins et al., 2008). Equally, the expansion of the ageing population has turned medical attention to cognitive decline and the onset of dementia (Ferri et al., 2005). These are all measures (see Chapter 2) and often change over time. In fact, a challenge in longitudinal analysis is being able to standardise a measurement taken at one point (maybe 10 or more years before) with one made later – or indeed a measure used in one study with another (Griffith et al., 2013).

Selecting your variables for analysis

There used to be a well-known phrase amongst those who were disparaging about the unthinking application of statistical techniques – 'rubbish in rubbish out'. What we have to do is distil the selection of variables for analysis so that they operationalise our analytical strategy in order to avoid any redundancy in our analysis. To use another metaphor, 'throwing the kitchen sink' at the problem will not lead to an elegant solution. Having a conceptual framework may help you to identify what is necessary for your understanding and why. Your reading and analysis of the literature will be an important first step in achieving this goal (refer to Chapter 3 in this volume). Every variable that you select has to have a good reason for being included in the analysis. If you are embarking on an empirical dissertation or project for the first time, you should consult previous dissertations in your subject area and closely examine the peer-reviewed literature in that domain. Spend time acquainting yourself with how others justify the selection of their variables for analysis, especially if they have been using the same data set.

Getting ready to analyse your data

Once we are satisfied with the conceptual coverage and resulting item selection for analysis, there are two important issues to consider before starting your data analysis: (1) checking the quality of our data and (2) deciding on whether or not we want to recode (reduce the categories in a response), derive or construct new variables (made up of the answers to two or more original questions).

1   *Data quality checks:* firstly, what is the quality of the data? What is the extent of unit non-response? This is when individuals are not present at a specific longitudinal time point. For example, they may have been present in 2000 but not in a later survey in the study. What is the extent of item missingness – often referred to as 'item non-response' (see Chapter 6 and later in this chapter). Secondly, are individuals consistent in the manner in which they respond to questions? Are question responses within range? (Eliminate codes which sit outside the range of question–response options as presented.)

2 *Merging data:* the attraction of analysing longitudinal data is that you are able to examine to what extent people's attitudes, behaviours, health status and living circumstances are influenced by their earlier life circumstances: for example, birth and childhood. The temporal ordering in the data provides opportunities to argue that current circumstances are the result of what happens before in life. Many people maintain that longitudinal data help us to make claims of cause and effect (see Chapter 2 and Volume 10). Typically, data will be available as cross-sectional sources at distinct time points, with a means of merging records via an individual identifier which never changes throughout the lifetime. So, in practical terms, we have to be sure that once we have identified the things that matter early in life, they are merged or combined with present-day or most recent outcomes in a single data file for our analysis. Essentially, this means creating longitudinal records: a record for an individual with repeat measures collected at particular time points. So each 'line' of the merged longitudinal data file contains every answer they have given at each stage of their life from birth to early old age.

3 *Data construction:* using longitudinal data, as we noted above, you may find that certain questions have been asked differently at two or more points during the life course. For instance, in the NCDS data set, sometimes respondents are asked for 'legal marital status' (single/married/divorced/widowed) and at other times for 'marital/partnership status' (the previous four categories plus separated/cohabiting). At other time points in the cohort member's life, there may be two separate questions: (1) 'Are you cohabiting?' and (2) 'Are you married?' For consistency, you may want to derive a series of variables which have exactly the same categories at each time point, using the information which is there in these available variables.

Analytical strategy

Always remember that 'there may be more than one way to crack a nut'. Getting to know your data will inevitably involve you in some patient reflection about how your item responses distribute themselves ('eyeballing' the marginal frequencies, more formally known as univariate analysis) and correlate with one another (looking for associations both expected and unexpected, known as bivariate analysis). You may well anticipate some of these out-turns, but some of the relationships in your data may surprise you.

Begin your analysis with your feet on the ground, in the sense of always being ready to return to the descriptives whenever your more sophisticated analyses (modelling as in later volumes) suggest there are still interesting avenues to explore before you can begin writing your narratives in conclusion of the analysis. The most important advice is to begin your analysis with a plan of action and share your ideas with your supervisor or research team members, but above all, remain flexible in your approach.

A case study illustration

Our illustration is an attempt to research childhood antecedents of well-being in early old age (50 years), using NCDS data from childhood and the 2008 follow-up when cohort members reach the grand old age of 50 years. Please note that this is 'real data', so percentages will not always be neat and tidy with no decimal places, and numbers will be as they are found to be, category or subsample sizes.

In the childhood of the NCDS cohort members, they and their parents were seen at birth and ages 7, 11 and 16 years – that is, three follow-ups to the initial birth survey, which are available as one consolidated childhood data set, henceforth referred to as 'ncds0123.sav'.

Outcome variables

Firstly, we look at possible 'outcome' variables at age 50 (equivalent of the dependent variable – see Chapter 2). The 2008 sweep of NCDS is rich in variables we could possibly use, with at least five sets of indicators available, but we highlight here just two of them:

1   CASP12 (control, autonomy, self-realisation and pleasure) a quality of life measure consisting of 12 items
2   Cognitive test results at age 50 (word recall, delayed word recall, animal-naming test and letter cancellation test)

For the purposes of this case study illustration our emphasis is solely upon aspects of data cleaning, consistency checking, and management. The job of predicting these outcomes or examining their inter-relationship follows with a working knowledge of regression analysis and access to on-line resources (see Concluding Section).

Early life influences on later outcomes

Our early life influences are chosen on the basis of the work of others who have tried to capture the social, biological and material circumstances of cohort members at birth along with various indicators of family life, cognitive performance and behaviour into the teenage years (e.g. Dodgeon et al., 2020). It is always important to be mindful of the fact that whilst longitudinal studies present the user with a rich and vast array of ways and means of characterising our sample members, our measures are typically 'proxies' for complex social and intellectual processes, and without in-depth qualitative data they will only signpost or indicate life circumstances. In formal terms, we will use our selected variables to predict the value of our outcomes using a technique described as multiple regression (Field, 2018).

In addition to gender, there are four variables which describe a child's social circumstances at birth along with some proxies for health. In childhood, 'family difficulties' is what we call a derived variable for the family when a child is aged 7 years. The variable uses responses to three items covering (1) finances, (2) housing and (3) employment. We also include whether or not a child was unhappy in school or spent time in care away from the family home. Cognitive performance is included at age 11 years: the time when a child is in transition from primary to secondary schooling. We also include three consecutive measures of social and emotional behaviour at ages 7, 11 and 16 years developed by Michael Rutter (Rutter et al., 1970). We will return to the properties of all of these variables in a later section, in terms of both their derivation and distributions. In order to simplify aspects of data handling, we will assume that all childhood variables have already been merged (ncds0123.sav), and we will concentrate on the steps involved in merging this data set with the data from sweep 8 (ncds_2008_followup.sav). To summarise then, we have identified the following variables:

Background at birth

- Parental social class variable
- Birthweight
- Mother smoked while pregnant or not
- Breastfed or not
- Sex

Childhood

- Family difficulties
- (Un)happy in school
- Cognitive ability aged 11 years
- Psychological distress at age 7 (Rutter7)
- Psychological distress at age 11 (Rutter11)
- Psychological distress at age 16 (Rutter16)

Let's get started on our preliminaries in order to prepare the data for analysis using SPSS version 26.0 (Field, 2018). To get these variables up on the screen, we first open the SPSS software and ask it to load the NCDS childhood data set (ncds0123.sav). We assume that you have already been to the UK Data Service website and downloaded the NCDS childhood data set to a folder on your computer called 'Userdata'. But first we need to discuss exactly how we are going to work in SPSS (user commands or drop-down menus).

SPSS drop-down menus or user commands?[i]

It's possible to specify all the steps in an SPSS analysis by issuing user commands in a 'syntax' file. This is also known as a 'command file' containing commands rather like instructions that are written in a programming language: here these commands are specific to SPSS. At any given time you would have three screens open:

1   Syntax screen (containing a file, say: 'syntax1.sps')
2   Output screen ('output1.spv')
3   Data editor screen (ncds0123.sav')

On the other hand, if you are just starting out to learn how to use SPSS and have not acquired any familiarity with SPSS syntax commands as yet, you can work with the drop-down menus (File/Edit/View/Data/Transform/Analyse and so on – see tabs on bar at top of screen). What's powerful about using SPSS is that these menu actions are automatically translated into command syntax so you can learn the 'language' as you become more confident about what you can achieve.

In this example, we'll use both, partly to illustrate the usefulness of getting to know SPSS commands. The reason for this is that, if you perform a successful analysis, you can keep a record of the commands which produced it: then, you can easily replicate that analysis with other variables or a different data set, simply by altering the variable names/ data set name in the saved syntax. You'll notice that the output file (output1.spv) keeps a note of every step you specified, translating the menu selections into the correct syntax.

So as we commence our example analysis, we first follow the choices as they appear in the drop-down menus (Figure 7.1), then, we note what the syntax looks like (copied from the output file if necessary).

Select 'File>Open>Data':

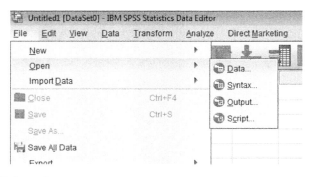

Figure 7.1   SPSS drop-down menus

Note: used with permission from IBM SPSS

---

[i]Here we are using SPSS version 26, but there may be some slight differences between earlier and later versions of SPSS.

Next, we specify we want to access the NCDS childhood data file (nds0123.sav; Figure 7.2):

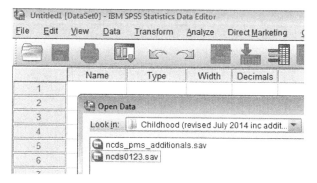

Figure 7.2 SPSS select data file

Note: used with permission from IBM SPSS

This brings up the data set in what is referred to as the 'Data Editor' screen. Look below as to its features. Firstly, there's a reminder in the top left-hand corner of the screen which confirms the name of the data file we are going to use (ncds0123.sav). Underneath the functions like 'View' and so on the icons are references to the nature of the data file. In the left-most column, there are consecutive numbers for each variable (1–15 and beyond). Next, we have the 'Name' of each variable as allocated by

	Name	Type	Width	Decimals	Label	Values
1	ncdsid	String	7	0	ncdsid serial nu...	None
2	n622	Numeric	8	0	0-3D Sex of child	{-1, Not kno...
3	n0region	Numeric	2	0	Region at PMS...	{-2, Not in P...
4	n1region	Numeric	2	0	Region at NCD...	{-2, Not in P...
5	n2region	Numeric	2	0	Region at NCD...	{-2, Not in P...
6	n3region	Numeric	2	0	Region at NCD...	{-2, Not in P...
7	n553	Numeric	8	0	0 Mother's age ...	{-1, NA}...
8	n545	Numeric	8	0	0 Mother's pres...	{-1, NA, inc...
9	n520	Numeric	8	0	0 Interval betwe...	{-1, NA}...
10	n490	Numeric	8	0	0 Socio-econo...	{-1, NA,no h...
11	n492	Numeric	8	0	0 Social class ...	{-1, NA,no h...
12	n494	Numeric	8	0	0 Husband's ag...	{-1, NA,no h...
13	n537	Numeric	8	0	0 Was mum at...	{-1, Dont Kn...
14	n524	Numeric	8	0	0 SEG matern...	{-1, Dont Kn...
15	n525	Numeric	8	0	0 SEG matern...	{-1, Dont Kn...

Figure 7.3 SPSS Data Editor screen

Note: used with permission from IBM SPSS

the researchers who originally deposited the data in the archive (e.g. n553) and its 'Type' ('String' or 'Numeric'). So for n553, we know that it consists of numbers only, whereas 'ncdsid' is a string variable which consists of numbers and letters. The next two columns tell us how many characters (letters and/or numbers) can be used for the values of the variable ('Width') and how many decimal places are to be used in the display of each numeric variable ('Decimals'). Notice that none of the variables illustrated are to be shown with any decimal places. The 'Label' column provides a longer description of the variable name, which is helpful when you are deciphering your output. The 'Values' column contains the range of codes for each variable. Clicking over any cell in that column opens the full range of codes for your inspection (see Figure 7.3).

Finally, the 'Missing' column indicates which values have been designated as always indicating no analysable data is present: for example, –1 or 999 are numeric codes conventionally used to indicate the 'residual' categories indicating 'not applicable' or 'not present at that sweep'.

Next, we open the data set which contains the 'outcome' variables: the NCDS8 follow-up (it's fine to have two data sets open at the same time).

Once more we select 'File>Open>Data', then specify the NCDS8 data set (Figure 7.4):

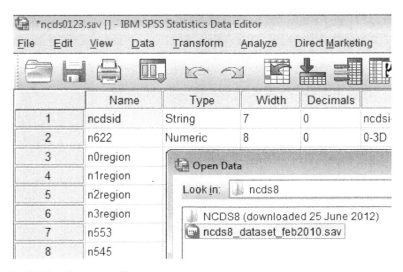

Figure 7.4 SPSS select data file

Note: used with permission from IBM SPSS

We now have two data sets open, as well as an output file and a (currently blank) syntax file. We can switch between these by the 'Window' tab (Figure 7.5).

We need to 'merge' the age 50 data set with the childhood data to form one big, longitudinally linked file.

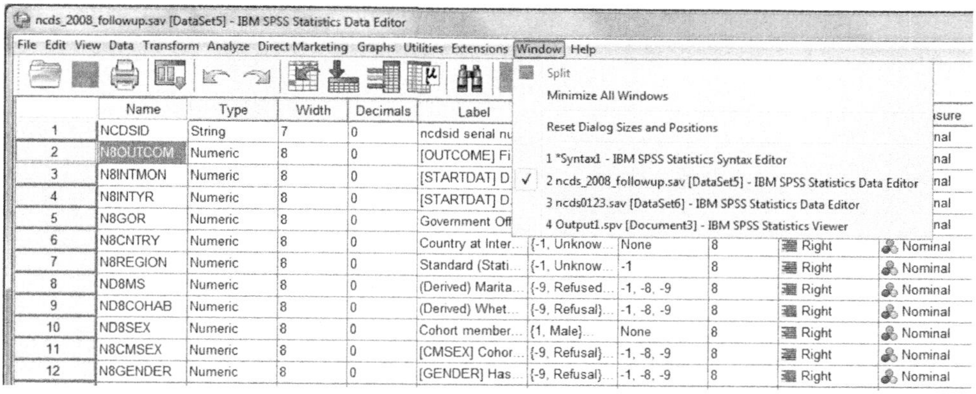

Figure 7.5 SPSS 'Window' tab

Note: used with permission from IBM SPSS

We first go back to the ncds0123.sav data file by clicking its name in the 'Window' drop-down menu shown in Figure 7.5; then, to merge it with ncds8, we click 'Data > Merge Files > Add Variables' (Figure 7.6):

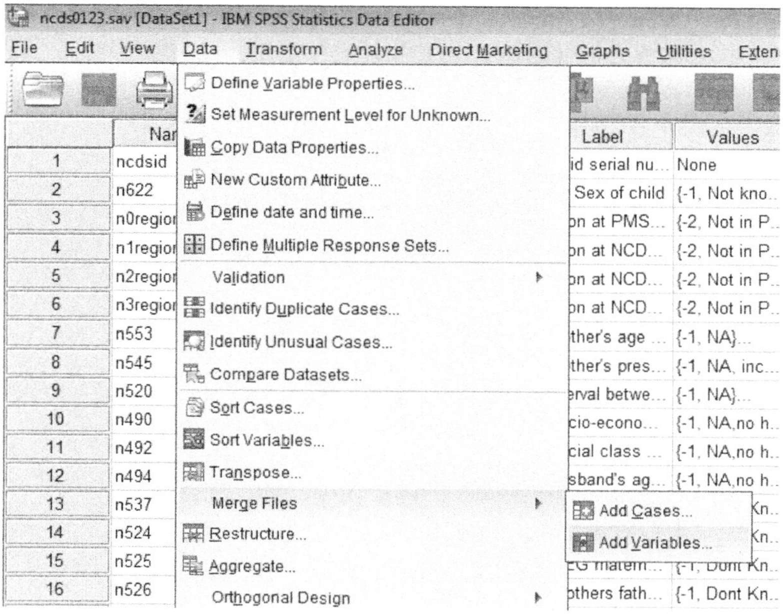

Figure 7.6 Merging data using SPSS 'Add Variables'

Note: used with permission from IBM SPSS

Notice that under the 'Merge Files' tab, we have two options both beginning with the word *add*. We can add variables to the same individuals or add cases (always with the same or common variables) to an existing set of cases. Remember that cases mean individuals here. Next, in the merging process, we say which (already-open) data set we want to be adding the variables from (ncds8; Figure 7.7):

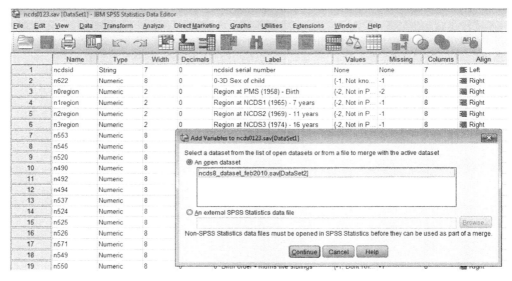

Figure 7.7 Merging data using SPSS 'Add Variables' continued

Note: used with permission from IBM SPSS

We get the screen as shown in Figure 7.8, which checks whether any variable names are duplicated between the two files being merged. The only duplicated

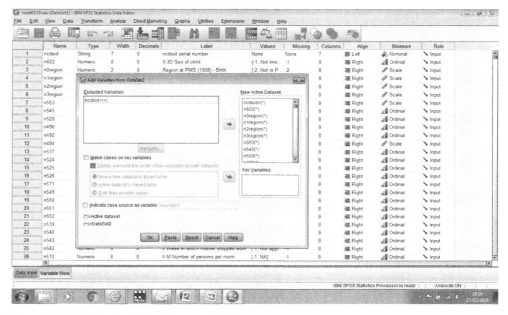

Figure 7.8 SPSS check duplicate variable names

Note: used with permission from IBM SPSS

variable is the individual case identifier 'ncdsid', which needs to be present in both files in order to have an exact match in both files ready for merging. Here it goes.

We highlight the 'ncdsid' variable and check the boxes marked 'Match cases on key variables' (here the matching is achieved by the value of 'ncdsid') and 'Cases are sorted in order of key variables . . .' (convention for ordering our data file in a tidy fashion; Figure 7.9).

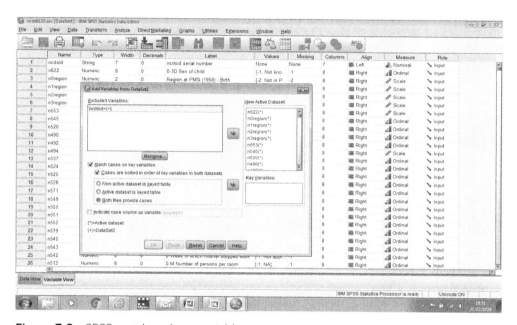

Figure 7.9   SPSS match and sort variable names

Note: used with permission from IBM SPSS

Then, we click the right arrow next to 'Key Variables', and 'ncdsid' is pasted into the 'Key Variables' box. Press 'OK', and the two files become merged. We have our longitudinal data file almost ready for analysis.

The merged file is still (for the time being) called ncds0123.sav. It's advisable to give it a new name, say ncds0123_8, so that we distinguish the new merged file from its component providers 'ncds0123' and 'ncds_8'. To achieve this, click 'File > Save as', and specify its new name.

We now don't need the ncds8 file, so you can use the 'Window' tab to go back to it and click 'File > Close'. You don't need to similarly 'close' the ncds0123 file in this procedure, because it has effectively 'become' ncds0123_8. But the original (unmerged) nds0123 file will still exist on your computer: it wasn't overwritten by anything, because you chose a new name for the merged data file.

We can now use that same 'Window' tab to make our way to the output file output1. spv, by selecting the third file in the list in the grey rectangle we see under 'Window' (Figure 7.10):

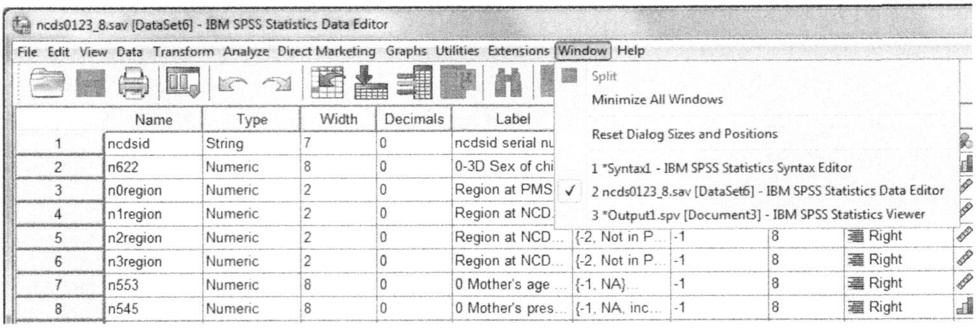

Figure 7.10   Saving your merged data file via the SPSS 'Window' tab

Note: used with permission from IBM SPSS

Here, in output1.spv, we see that all these drop-down menu selections that we made have been recorded as a series of SPSS syntax commands. This happens automatically: each command has a very specific form, always terminated by a full stop. As you get used to saving syntax files, you should become familiar with their form and function:

GET FILE='C:\Userdata\ncds0123.sav'.

MATCH FILES /FILE=*

/FILE='C:\Userdata\ncds8_dataset_feb2010.sav'

/BY ncdsid.

EXECUTE

SAVE OUTFILE='C:\Userdata\ncds0123_8.sav'.

It's a good idea to copy and paste this syntax into a syntax file that you save for future use. Simply running that syntax will enable you to merge files quickly, by substituting their names for these.

Now, it's time to begin checking the quality of our data. Firstly, we'll examine the extent of data loss as a result of either individuals dropping out of the study over time (attrition) or some questions (items) not being answered by individuals, or answers classed as 'missing' (see paragraph above about values shown in the 'Missing' column): for example, the answer to 'What is your husband's occupation?' might be '–1 not applicable' because the cohort member hasn't got a husband.

Missing data

Looking at the merged data file produced above, we note that there are many more cases with valid data for the earlier (childhood) sweeps than the later ones. This gradual attrition of the survey population is shown graphically in Figure 7.11.

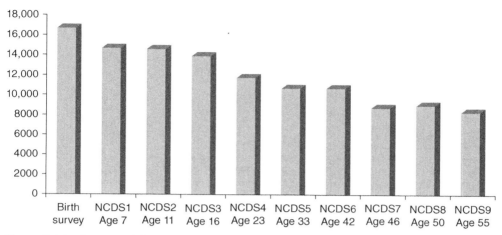

Figure 7.11 Attrition of the National Child Development Study survey population, 1958–2013

Historically, at the birth survey, 17,415 babies were included, representing 98% of all the births in Great Britain in that survey week. Attempts were made in subsequent sweeps to contact the remaining 2%, and also to include those born abroad in the 1958 survey week who became immigrants to Great Britain by 1974 and were identified in schools at ages 7, 11 or 16. So a further 537 cases were added in 1965 (age 7), 297 added in 1969 (age 11) and 303 added in 1974 (age 16). A further 6 were picked up at age 23 or 33, making a total of 18,558 cohort members who were ever seen during their lives and the life of the birth cohort study.

Nevertheless, the additional 1143 cohort members (18,558 minus 17,415) were not enough to compensate for the gradual loss to follow-up of about 2000 children in the 1965 and 1969 surveys, which by 1974 was nearly 3000 down on the original 17,415 babies of 1958.

Going forward to age 50, we see from Figure 7.11 that only 9790 members remained in the survey, representing 56% of the original number, or, more accurately, 52.8% of all the 18,558 people who were ever part of the survey at any time. Nevertheless, the attrition pattern is not monotonic: some people reconnect to the survey after missing one or two follow-ups, so the age 50 total is actually slightly higher than at age 46 (which was 9534).

In our merged 'Childhood-plus-age 50' data set, for any cohort member who was not present at the age 50 survey you will see that all the 'age 50' variables will be shown as having missing values for that case. There will also be missing values for any instances where a cohort member present at age 50 has failed to complete or respond to a particular question. The former cases make up 'unit non-response' and the latter 'item non-response'. There are ways of compensating for data loss by a combination of weighting and imputation (Kalton & Flores-Cervantes, 2003; Mostafa & Wiggins, 2015), but for this example, we will simply analyse those cases that have complete information.

We do this in two stages: we first delete any cases where there are no age 50 variables. Secondly, we merge the cases containing age 50 variables with the childhood data. The first variable listed in the age 50 data set will help us in this task: N8OUTCOM indicates what happened when the fieldwork interviewer visited to try to see the cohort member at age 50 (Table 7.1):

Table 7.1 Final outcome for household interview

		Frequency	Percent	Valid Percent	Cumulative Percent
Valid	110 productive interview	9758	52.6	99.7	99.7
	130 proxy interview	22	00.1	00.2	99.9
	210 partial productive interview	10	00.1	00.1	100.0
	Total	9790	52.8	100.0	
Missing	System	8768	47.2		
Total		18,558	100.0		

Within the 18,558 cases of the combined data set, there are 9790 cases where an age 50 interview took place (in 10 of these cases, only 'partially productive': i.e. the interview was abandoned at a certain point; in another 22 interviews, a 'proxy' respondent answered for the cohort member as they themselves were unable to answer because of disability or infirmity).

The remaining 8768 cases in Table 7.1 don't have a value at all, because no age 50 interview took place. So they are like the cases given special values of −1 or 999 in the 'Missing' column in the 'Data Editor' screen we discussed in the section above. But because they've not been given any values at all, the SPSS software refers to them as 'system-missing'. In SPSS-speak, 'SYSMIS' is a powerful indicator and a reminder that you need to check the marginal frequencies of all of your variables before you start any serious analysis. This is particularly the case when you need to recode or create new variables (derive) from existing variables (more to follow).

If we delete all cases where N8OUTCOM is missing (i.e. select only cases where N8OUTCOM has a positive value), this will leave us with a merged data set containing just the 9790 cases where at least some of the age 50 interview questions were answered. To achieve this, we will use a handy option within SPSS called 'Select if', which allows us to cut down the size of the data set according to any specified condition (e.g. we could select just those in certain geographical regions): in this case, we select cases where there was a genuine interview at age 50 years and reject all the rest.

We can do this with drop-down menus as follows: we click 'Data > Select Cases' (shown as six steps beginning with Figure 7.12):

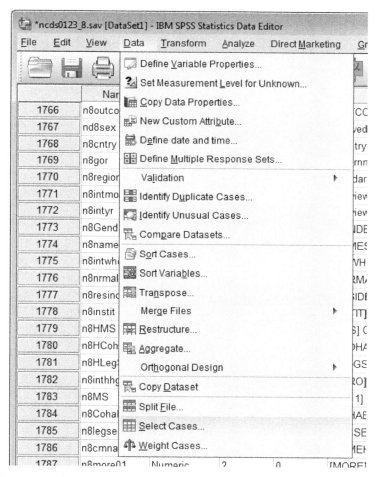

Figure 7.12 SPSS Select Cases 1

Note: Used with permission from IBM SPSS.

Another dialogue box opens up. Inside this 'Select Cases' dialogue box, we see a list of all the variables in our merged data file ncds0123_8. The dialogue box wants us to specify a 'condition' involving one of our variables. We want the condition to be that N8OUTCOM has a positive value.

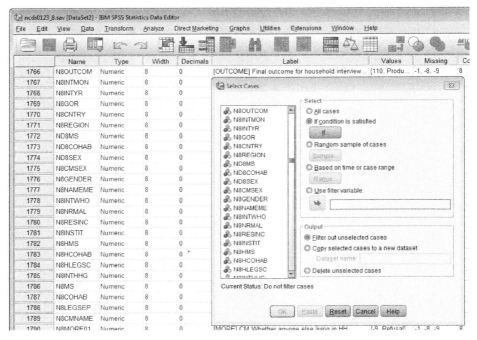

Figure 7.13 SPSS Select Cases 2

Note. Used with permission from IBM SPSS.

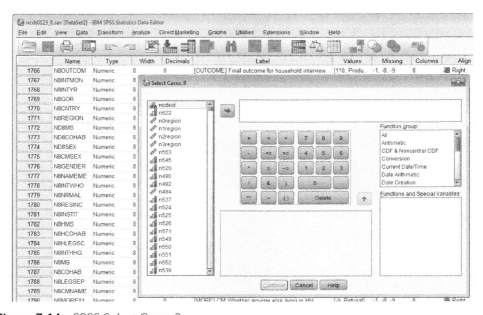

Figure 7.14 SPSS Select Cases 3

Note. Used with permission from IBM SPSS.

So we check 'If condition is satisfied' and click the tab labelled 'If' (Figure 7.13).

On clicking 'If', another dialogue box appears: we are invited to select one of the variables (Figure 7.14).

We select N8OUTCOM by scrolling down the list till we find it; then, click the arrow by the white box, and that variable name is pasted into the white box. We want the condition to be that the variable has a positive value (i.e. >0), so we click the tab under the white box, labelled '>', and also click the '0' tab (Figure 7.15):

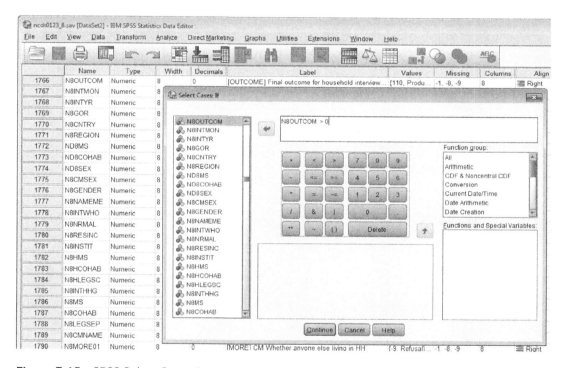

Figure 7.15   SPSS Select Cases 4

Note. Used with permission from IBM SPSS.

Then, we click the 'Continue' tab and we're back to the 'Select Cases' dialogue box (Figure 7.16).

Finally, we want the selected cases to be copied to a new file, so we check 'Copy selected cases to a new data set', which we'll call 'ncd20123_8_complete', and we type that name in the white box and click 'OK' (Figure 7.17).

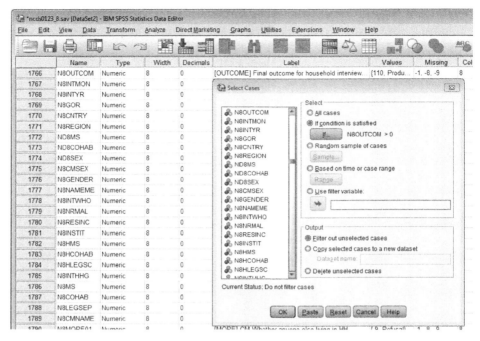

Figure 7.16 SPSS Select Cases 5

Note. Used with permission from IBM SPSS.

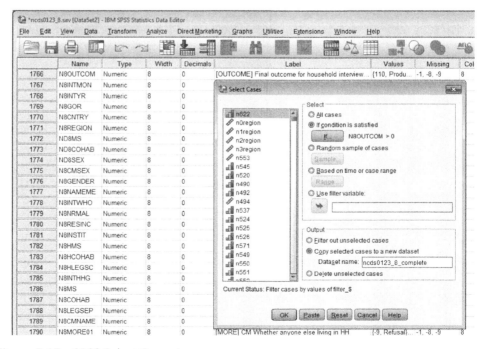

Figure 7.17 SPSS Select Cases 6

Note. Used with permission from IBM SPSS.

Reducing our data set by using the drop-down menus achieves our goal and has the advantage of introducing you to the depths of SPSS: but we could have achieved the same result by typing in just two lines of syntax (Figure 7.18) into our 'syntax1' file, highlighting those two lines and pressing the green 'Run selection' arrow:

Select if (N8OUTCOM >0).
Save outfile='C:\Userdata\ncds0123_8_complete.sav'.

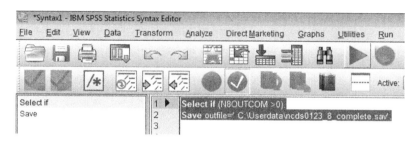

Figure 7.18   SPSS syntax file

Note. Used with permission from IBM SPSS.

So we now have our new, edited-down data set containing childhood variables and age 50 variables for all those present at the age 50 survey.

Our next step will be to examine the extent of any missingness for the items in our data set, together with the range defined by the lowest to the highest value codes (the minimum, maximum values if you prefer). These are listed in Table 7.2. Beyond checking the legitimacy of variable ranges, there will often be the opportunity to check that questions have been answered in a logical manner. These are known as 'consistency checks'. Typically, they occur where certain questions only apply if a condition is met: for example, questions that might be applicable only for mothers who smoked during pregnancy. To be able to construct consistency checks of this type, you need to get to know the questionnaires before you can implement the check. This process of familiarisation of what items of information are available is time well spent. There is one variable in the selection that is present in Table 7.2 that we have included for the sole purpose of illustrating the opportunity to carry out a consistency check. This is the variable 'n545 Mother's present marital status'.

A standardised score (see Volume 3) is simply the original score minus its mean and then divided by its standard deviation. Hence, the description is 'standardised', which means you can combine several scores as they are all measured on a common scale (with a mean of zero).

Table 7.2 List of variables in 'ncds0123_8_complete' by percentage missing and range of values based on 9790 cohort members aged 50 years in 2008

Variable Description	Variable Name	Percent Missing	Minimum, Maximum Codes
Birth characteristics			
Mother's husband's social class	N492	5.2	−1, 12
Mother's present marital status	N545	5.2	−1, 5
Birthweight (ounces)	N646	5.6	36, 204
Mother smoked while pregnant or not	N639	6.5	1, 4
Breastfed or not	N222	12.3	1, 4
Sex	N622	0	1, 2
Childhood			
Family difficulties			
Housing	N314	12.5	0, 2
Financial	N315	12.5	0, 2
Unemployment	N324	12.6	0, 2
Happiness at school	N115	12.3	1, 4
Cognitive ability at age 11 years	Cog11Zsum	13.7	−13.31, 8.67 (sum of 4 standardised scores)
Psychological distress at age 7 years	Rutter7	8.5	0, 24
Psychological distress at age 11 years	Rutter11	6.8	0, 25
Psychological distress at age 16 years	Rutter16	9.6	0, 25
Age 50 years			
CASP +	CASP12sum	11.9	2, 36
Cognitive test score +	Cog50Zsum	4.1	−12.00, 9.87 (sum of 4 standardised scores)

Note. '+' indicates that both CASP12sum and the Cognitive test score are summative indices based on the original variables. The acronym CASP labels the four item domains where C= control, A=autonomy, S= self-realisation and P= pleasure.

The level of missingness for individual items or derived variables (created from a group of individual items) varies between 0% and 13.7%. The simplest approach to handling this issue is to delete anybody (case) with a missing value on one or more variables. This is referred to as 'listwise deletion' and could seriously reduce your sample size, and that's what we're going to do here. This action could bias our results, and it would be worth investing some time and effort in 'filling in' or imputing any missing values (Mostafa & Wiggins, 2015). SPSS allows you to explore the pattern of missingness in your data and/or select an imputation procedure. It's recommended that you build this into your analytical strategy once you feel more confident about the basis upon which missing values are 'filled in'.

Before we carry out a listwise deletion, we declare which values we wish to be regarded as 'missing' for each of the 15 variables in Table 7.2. Some of them are never missing (e.g. N622 'sex': a characteristic recorded at birth for all cohort members), and others (e.g. the summed scores CASP12, Cog11Zscore and Cog50Zscore) are either a valid number or they're 'system-missing', so we don't need to declare missing values for these.

The following syntax declares the missing values of the variables where '−1' is meant to be regarded as missing:

missing values n646 n639 n222 n314 n315 n324 n115 Rutter7 Rutter11 Rutter16 (−1).

Having declared the missing values, we once more use the 'Select if' command for each variable in Table 7.2, to delete all cases with missing values:

```
Select if (not(missing(n492))).
Select if (not(missing(n646))).
Select if (not(missing(n639))).
Select if (not(missing(n222))).
Select if (not(missing(n622))).
Select if (not(missing(n314))).
Select if (not(missing(n315))).
Select if (not(missing(n324))).
Select if (not(missing(n115))).
Select if (not(missing(Cog11Zsum))).
Select if (not(missing(Rutter7))).
Select if (not(missing(Rutter11))).
Select if (not(missing(Rutter16))).
Select if (not(missing(CASP12sum))).
Select if (not(missing(Cog50Zsum))).
```

From our 9790 cases in the data set 'ncds0123_8_complete', this leaves us with 5795 cases with no missing values in any of the variables in our analysis. This implies that we have abandoned 3995 of the cases because they each lack the response to at least one item. These cases have what we call partial information, and given that they represent 41% (i.e. {(9790-5795)/9790}*100%) of the age 50 sample, it only serves to emphasise the need to carry out imputation whenever you are handling large samples. We save these in a new data set which we call 'ncds0123_8_listw-del':

Save outfile= 'C:\Userdata\ncds0123_8_listw_del.sav'.

Before we carry out any analysis using this data set, we are going to illustrate two further checks which typically have general applicability in any data checking or cleaning task: (1) consistency checks and (2) checks on the creation of derived variables. Once we have illustrated these practices, we will consider in a little more detail the common practice of recoding variables – that is, reducing the number of categories, or degree of continuity, into a smaller number of more manageable categories. Of course, it could be argued that this is like throwing away information, for example, reclassifying exact birthweights measured in grams into 'lightweight, average or heavyweight' babies. We will return to the use of recodes once we have considered the practice of consistency checking.

A consistency check is where we ensure that the presence of a code in any field of data for a variable is to be found according to the rules of the questionnaire design. Typically, this is where there are 'filters' in the questionnaire such as 'If respondent married, then ask next question, otherwise skip to question n+1'.

In our current analysis, since we have a variable (n492) 'Mother's husband's social class', it's a good idea to check this against the mother's marital status (variable n545) to see what happens where there is no husband (Tables 7.3, 7.4 and 7.5).

To get frequency counts of both variables, we can type this command into our 'syntax1' file:

Frequencies n492 n545.

We execute this command by highlighting it and pressing the green 'execute' arrow. These counts then appear in the output screen:

Table 7.3 Social class mother's husband (UK's General Register Office classification (GRO) 1951)

		Frequency	Percent	Valid Percent	Cumulative Percent
Valid	−1 NA, no husband	111	1.9	1.9	1.9
	2 I	269	4.6	4.6	6.6
	3 II	830	14.3	14.3	20.9
	4 III	3372	58.2	58.2	79.1
	5 IV	659	11.4	11.4	90.4
	6 V	433	7.5	7.5	97.9
	9 students	7	0.1	0.1	98.0
	10 dead or away	1	0.0	0.0	98.1
	12 single, no husband	113	1.9	1.9	100.0
	Total	5795	100.0	100.0	

Table 7.4 Mother's present marital status

		Frequency	Percent	Valid Percent	Cumulative Percent
Valid	−1 NA, incomplete information	1	00.0	00.0	00.0
	1 separated, divorced and widowed	43	00.7	00.7	00.8
	2 stable union	6	00.1	00.1	00.9
	3 twice married	6	00.1	00.1	01.0
	4 married	5626	97.1	97.1	98.1
	5 unmarried	113	01.9	01.9	100.0
	Total	5795	100.0	100.0	

'For a useful consistency check, we now crosstabulate these variables against each other, by issuing the command 'Crosstabs n492 by nn545

Table 7.5 Crosstabulation of social class of mother's husband (GRO 1951) by Mother's present marital status (n545 0)

Count

			n545 0 Mother's present marital status						
		−1 NA, incomplete information	1 separated, divorced and widowed	2 stable union	3 twice married	4 married	5 unmarried	Total
n492 0 Social class mother's husband (GRO 1951)	−1 NA, no husband	1	22	2	0	**86**	0	111
	2 I	0	0	0	0	269	0	269
	3 II	0	1	0	1	828	0	830
	4 III	0	13	3	2	3354	0	3372
	5 IV	0	4	1	0	654	0	659
	6 V	0	2	0	3	428	0	433
	9 students	0	0	0	0	7	0	7
	10 dead or away	0	1	0	0	0	0	1
	12 single, no husband	0	0	0	0	0	113	113
Total		1	43	6	6	5626	113	5795

We see that, as expected, most of the 5626 cases where the mother is 'married' have a valid social class for mother's husband, with 7 husbands being students. We have

86 cases (highlighted), where the mother is married but the husband's social class is labelled '–1 not applicable or no husband'. So we conclude that in these cases, there is a husband but he hasn't got a social class code I to V for some other reason. One suspects all those 86 cases were simply coded 'not applicable' because the husband was unemployed or sick.

We also note from the cross-tabulation (Table 7.5) that half of the 43 cases where n545 indicates the mother is 'separated/divorced/widowed' do we have a valid 'husband's social class' code (consistent with being 'separated'); one is coded 'dead or away', consistent with the widowhood status, and the other 22 are coded '–1 Not applicable or no husband', consistent with being divorced.

All 113 mothers coded '5 unmarried' are also coded '12 single, no husband', which is fine. Those coded '3 twice married' all have a valid husband's social class code, which is also fine, and finally, we see that four of the six 'stable union' cases seem to treat the stable union as effectively being a marriage (valid social class code), whereas the other four treat it as '–1 NA, no husband'.

So our consistency check has shown that there's nothing much to worry about and taught us a little more about the detail of how potentially ambiguous cases were coded.

Recoding and deriving variables

We turn now to the issue of recoding variables (reducing or relabelling the categories in a variable); we illustrate this by looking at the three variables which we want to combine under the heading of 'family difficulties': (1) n314 'housing', (2) n315 'finance' and (3) n324 'unemployment'. We are simply going to create a derived variable which counts exactly how many family difficulties have been reported, thus holding the values 0, 1, 2 or 3 (Table 7.6).

We get their frequency distributions with this command:

Fre n314 n315 n324.
(note that the word *frequencies* can be abbreviated to just *fre*)

Table 7.6   Family difficulties in housing, finances and unemployment

		n314 1P Family difficulties: housing			
		Frequency	**Percent**	**Valid Percent**	**Cumulative Percent**
Valid	1 do not know	285	4.9	4.9	4.9
	2 yes	337	5.8	5.8	10.7
	3 no	5173	89.3	89.3	100.0
	Total	5795	100.0	100.0	

continues over page...

n315 1P Family difficulties: financial				
		Frequency	Percent	Valid Percent	Cumulative Percent
Valid	1 do not know	550	9.5	9.5	9.5
	2 yes	333	5.7	5.7	15.2
	3 no	4912	84.8	84.8	100.0
	Total	5795	100.0	100.0	

n324 1P Family difficulties: unemployment				
		Frequency	Percent	Valid Percent	Cumulative Percent
Valid	1 do not know	371	6.4	6.4	6.4
	2 yes	145	2.5	2.5	8.9
	3 no	5279	91.1	91.1	100.0
	Total	5795	100.0	100.0	

We see that there are three valid codes, including 'do not know' (this is because the question was answered by the family's health visitor, who would usually be aware of these types of difficulties but may not have enough information to form an opinion). If we wanted to create a 'score' of family difficulties and avoid the problem of what to do about 'do not knows', it would work best if we first recoded these variables so that 'yes' was coded 1 and both 'no' and 'do not know' were coded 0; so for each of the types of family difficulties, we are only increasing the score when one of the answers is 'yes'.

Using the SPSS 'Recode' command, this process is very simple and can be applied to all three variables at once:

Recode n314 n315 n324 (1=0)(2=1)(3=0).

This command asks SPSS to go through all three variables and change every code 1 to '0', every code 2 to '1' and every code 3 to '0'.

But we also need to relabel the values for all three variables. We use the 'Value labels' command:

Value labels n314 n315 n324
0 'No or Do not Know'.
1 'Yes'.

So we now have (e.g. for n314) as follows (Table 7.7):

Table 7.7 Family difficulties: housing

		Frequency	Percent	Valid Percent	Cumulative Percent
Valid	0 no or do not know	5458	94.2	94.2	94.2
	1 yes	337	5.8	5.8	100.0
	Total	5795	100.0	100.0	

We have now arrived at the point where we can use our three recoded variables to illustrate our final stage of data preparation before the analysis properly begins: the creation of a derived variable.

Referring back to Table 7.2, we have our three variables above grouped under the one category 'family difficulties'. If we wanted to construct one variable which reflected the degree of difficulties the family was under, we could add the three (recoded) values, which would give us a minimum score of 0 (no difficulties) and a maximum of 3 (all three difficulties).

We can construct a new variable 'famdiffs' whose value is the sum of all our recoded variables:

Compute famdiffs=n314+n315+n324.

This gives us the derived variable named 'famdiffs' with a score from 0 to 3 (Table 7.8):

Table 7.8 A count of the number of family difficulties (famdiffs)

		Frequency	Percent	Valid Percent	Cumulative Percent
Valid	0	5185	89.5	89.5	89.5
	1	439	7.6	7.6	97.0
	2	137	2.4	2.4	99.4
	3	34	0.6	0.6	100.0
	Total	5795	100.0	100.0	

Note that we have no missing values in the derived variable: having performed our listwise deletion, each of the constituent variables (n315, n315 and n324) had exactly the same number of valid codes (5795). In adding the three scores together, if any one of the three is missing, SPSS produces a missing value for the total. But we don't have to worry about any such discrepancy, because our listwise deletion harmonised the exact number of valid cases.

There are quite a few derived variables in our data, most notably the cognitive scores, psychological distress scores and the age 50 outcomes. For instance, the CASP score is the sum of 12 scores, each of '0, 1, 2, 3' defined to represent (as the acronym CASP indicates) the four aspects of quality of life labelled control, autonomy, self-realisation and pleasure.

In this way, the maximum or peak value of quality of life is a total score of '36' for a wholly positive 50-year-old with no misgivings about life. In general, we call these measures 'summative indices'. Let's now have a look at how these scores are distributed by inspecting their shape, arithmetic mean (lay term would be average) and median (lay term would be the middle-most score) in Table 7.9:

Looking at the shape of the frequency distributions in Table 7.9 below, we see that some variables have a symmetrical distribution (notably, cognitive test scores at ages 11 and age 50) and others are less symmetrical in shape. Imagine that we had paper cutouts of the distributions; then, we could demonstrate what we mean by symmetry as when we fold the distribution along its axis of symmetry (the vertical line positioned at the mean) we would hardly get any overlap. We refer to distributions where there are departures from symmetry as being 'skewed'. If the mean exceeds the median, a distribution is said to be 'skewed to the right' (essentially the mean pulls the tail of the distribution to the right of the image), and 'skewed to the left', where the mean is smaller than the median. Consequently, psychological distress at ages 7, 11 and 16 are skewed towards the right, and CASP is skewed to the left.

The reason for this is that psychological distress scores are measuring signs of how unhappy the child is on a scale of 1 to 14, adding up points according to 14 questions such as 'Is the child restless/squirmy/fidgety?' 'Does he or she get bullied at school?' Thankfully, most children are not very unhappy, and so their mother doesn't answer 'yes' to more than about three or four of these questions. It's rare for a child to have a score of 14, but very common to have a score of zero. So this is why we have a little skewness to the right, with a pronounced 'high bar' (especially at 16 years) indicating a lot of people with a score of exactly zero. Conversely, the CASP Quality-of-Life score is slightly skewed to the left with a tiny minority reporting low levels of quality of life.

In contrast, with the cognitive test scores, there are as many people getting a 'below average' score as those getting 'above average', and the distribution 'tails off' at both ends in a similar way (i.e. there are very few people getting a 100% score and very few getting a zero cognitive score). So this leads to symmetry rather than skewness.

Table 7.9   Univariate properties of key derived variables

Variable Description With Mean and Median Values	Percent Frequency Distribution
Cognitive test score aged 11 years .1751, .2484 (sum of four standardised scores)	
Psychological distress at age 7 years 6.09, 6.0	
Psychological distress at age 11 years 5.73, 5.0	
Psychological distress at age 16 years 3.29, 2.0	
Cognitive test score aged 50 years .1202, .0818 (sum of four standardised scores)	
CASP Quality of Life score 26.17, 27.0	

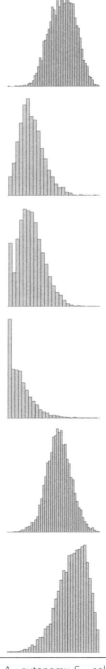

Note. The label 'CASP' refers to the four item domains C = control, A= autonomy, S = self-realisation and P = pleasure.

Conclusions

As we suggested in Chapter 3, it is important to immerse yourself in the literature and ascertain what other research has been carried out in the area you're interested in. If there's readily available data, get to know the sources, the questionnaire and the limitations of any secondary data when selecting variables for your analysis. Above all, what we want to emphasise is the importance of checking the quality of your data before you begin your analysis. Inspect the variable coding and the presence of missing data. Have a strategy for managing your data for analysis, together with a rationale for any recoding or the construction of derived variables. Avoid rushing into sophisticated analysis (made easy by menu-driven software) which can be misleading if there are aberrant data values in your data set. Our case study illustration has been developed in order to take you through some fairly detailed aspects of data management using a large and complex data set using powerful statistical software. The idea is to provide a 'real-world' encounter with data analysis. We have only brought you to the exciting point of departure where you can begin your statistical analysis. Once you feel confident to embark on this part of the journey (ideally, after reading Volumes 2, 3, 7 and 8), we recommend that you consult the extension of this chapter as contained in the online resources (https://study.sagepub.com/quantitativekit). Meanwhile, please hold on to the fundamental aspect of learning to be a competent data analyst – namely, 'not to run before you can walk'. Begin by making friends with your data by inspecting frequency distributions and associations between pairs of variables and, like in any friendship, give yourself time to 'hang out' together. Numbers cannot stand alone.

Chapter Summary

- Secondary data refers to both numbers (quantitative) and words (qualitative). Typically, for the purpose of social research, these data will refer to surveys and administrative data which are deposited in accessible archives, but increasingly, during the 21st century, new social media also provide new sources of 'big data'.
- This chapter is built around a case study of a longitudinal survey which carefully details the steps that a secondary analyst will tread in order to realise a plan of analysis. The emphasis is upon quality checking selected variables including the assessment of missing data, recoding and deriving new variables and merging data from key stages of the life course in order to explore the impact of childhood and adolescence on later life well-being and cognitive functioning.

Acknowledgements

This chapter was co-authored with Brian Dodgeon, Senior Research Officer, Centre for Longitudinal Studies, UCL – Social Research Institute, London, UK (www.cls.ucl.ac.uk).

Further Reading

Johnston, M. P. (2014). Secondary data analysis: A method of which the time has come. *Qualitative and Quantitative Methods in Libraries, 3*(3), 619–626. www.qqml-journal.net/index.php/qqml/article/view/169

There is no doubt that as technology advances the range of data available for secondary analysis will continue to grow exponentially. If you happen to be embarking upon a dissertation, the rich resources available in data archives may present attractive opportunities for you to become a secondary analyst. You can refer to this helpful article.

MacInnes, J. (2016). *An introduction to secondary data analysis with IBM SPSS statistics.* Sage.

John MacInnes (author of *The SAGE Quantitative Research Kit*, Volume 3) has written an immensely useful guide for those of you who elect to take up secondary data analysis in the near future.

8

THE SOCIAL CONTEXT OF QUANTITATIVE RESEARCH

Chapter Overview

Introduction

We began this volume by noting that all social research is located within the political and social worlds in which it is carried out. Not only is the process of research a social act, but its motivation through choices of things to investigate is also socially motivated, and the consequences of its findings have social effects. Critics of quantitative research will claim that this social embeddedness undermines our claims to be scientific, because value freedom is impossible to achieve when values determine its direction and execution at every stage. A moral position sometimes follows from this, that quantitative methods reflect and further a hegemonic social structure.

This is, in our view, simplistic, but equally is the one that sees the only important social effects as arising from the **ethics** of how we treat our respondents. Though this is important, it is the narrow view of ethics committees, as much concerned about litigation as ethical scientific research. This view treats quantitative methods as if they are socially neutral. It is true that these positions are perhaps expressed in more nuanced terms, but they serve to illustrate two pole positions about the social situatedness (or not!) of quantitative methods. For us, the question of values, context and ethics are closely entwined, and in this chapter our aim is to sketch out (and it can be no more than that, in the space available) a holistic approach to the relationship between scientific inquiry, social context and ethical research.

In this chapter, we do three things. Firstly, we explore the social and political context of social research, but specifically how can socially situated research be objective? Secondly, we examine the ethics of inquiry, once the research has been proposed, and in the final section, we bring together political, ethical and methodological issues in a checklist of what to look for in research – how to assess good and bad research.

Where does social inquiry come from?

The philosopher of science Karl Popper used to ask his students to look around the classroom and tell him what they observed during a minute of silence. Unsurprisingly, this elicited several and varied responses. As Popper noted, this was not just about observing different things but also the cognitive priorities that led to the observations. He might also have added (perhaps stating the obvious) that what they observed would be limited to what there was to observe in the room.

This is a good analogy for social research – it is those things that interest us, or are seen as societal priorities, that we research. This is equally true of the natural sciences, and an excellent example is that geologists know more about oil-bearing shales than any other rock, because the geology of oil-bearing shales has been a scientific priority ever since society wanted oil (Proctor, 1991, p. 10). This is equally true in social science. In December 2017, the funding opportunities of the UK Economic and Social Research Council (ESRC) contained the following headings (www.esrc.ac.uk/funding/funding-opportunities):

Addressing the challenge of antimicrobial resistance in India
New models of sustainable development

Understanding of the impacts of hydrometeorological hazards in South East Asia

Dementia research initiative 2018 – prevention, interventions and care delivery

Climate change priority

These are not the totality of what the ESRC was, is or will fund, but they are a snapshot of priorities at a moment in time, and these particular priorities are organised around the theme of environment and sustainability. They could have been other things, and indeed each year the ESRC, as do other funding bodies in the UK and other countries, sets their funding priorities for that year. In the past, priorities have included governance, education and health. Indeed, for a period in the late 1990s and 2000s, socio-medical research received a comparatively large slice of UK funding, to the point where in some years the medical sociology research group of the British Sociological Association (MedSoc) had more delegates attending its conference than its parent body. To a great extent, priorities will exist across all levels of research from large centres to PhD research. This matters, because, as we said in Chapter 4, all research requires resources. The most important of these is money, to pay for staff and, where appropriate, other costs such as fieldwork. Consequently, what is researched is largely the result of what is funded, and what is funded is decided by a relatively narrow range of people in government, the third sector and in the senior echelons of universities. We are not saying that this is either a good thing or a bad thing, and possibly it is inevitable in any society where funding decisions must be narrowed to priorities, and almost by definition, priority decisions can only be eventually made by a minority, however widely they consult.

In this volume (and indeed in the *The SAGE Research Quantitative Kit*), we refer to large data sets which have been 'curated' not with a specific research question or questions in mind but rather as resources. These might include the census (in several countries), in the UK *Understanding Society*, the *Millennium Cohort Study*, the *Labour Force Survey* and the *National Child Development Study* (see the analysis example in Chapter 7, amongst many others) and in the USA *The National Longitudinal Study of Youth* or *The General Social Survey*. Because they are not answering any specific questions, they might be seen to be more scientifically 'neutral', and indeed it is true that they can be used to answer a huge variety of research questions, some of which may be potentially politically 'opposed'. But they are not value free, because someone or a group of people must decide which questions are asked. In long-running or panel studies, despite a lot of continuity of questions, some topics (and questions) change over time. Take, for example, the existence of certain facilities available to households and asked in the England and Wales census over the decades. In 1971, respondents were asked if they had access to running water, cooking facilities, indoor toilets and bathrooms. By 1981, this became indoor toilets and bathrooms, and by 1991 this was dropped in favour of a question about central heating (see Dale & Marsh, 1993). In these decades, housing conditions changed and the earlier questions became irrelevant, as virtually everyone had those facilities. At the time of writing, 95%[i] of dwellings in the UK had central heating, and this too will become less useful as a question. Though, over time, these measures have stood in as 'proxy' for relative levels of poverty in households.

So what is funded and what is asked in every study is socially situated and more often than not the result of political priorities in given societies.

Social situatedness is not only an important consideration as to what places a research topic on to the agenda and the research questions it leads to but also an aspect of measurement itself. How we measure things like sex/gender, social class and ethnicity are what one of us has termed *sociological variables* (Williams, 2003), that is what they measure as changes between one time and another, or one place and another.

The measurement of social class has long been controversial (Payne et al., 1996), because for one thing it mostly represents socio-economic status usually measured through occupation type. Can occupation stand in for class relations and the cultural component of class? We will not try to answer that question but merely state it as an example of the challenge of social measurement.

At the time of writing, debate has begun about the measurement of sex/gender (e.g. see Fugard, 2020[ii]; Sullivan, 2020). Sociologists, for a long time, have pointed out that biological sex cannot stand in for the complex set of characteristics that gender is. Survey researchers have responded by saying that the categories male/female are not meant to be measures of gender but only biological sex, and moreover, sex (as measured) remains an important predictor of male/female life chances. But a growing debate about transgender indicators has led to calls for a third (or more) categories. Possibly a third category would be useful, though it brings us back to the question of whether we are then measuring sex or gender? It is perhaps less of

---

[i]www.statista.com/statistics/289137/central-heating-in-households-in-the-uk.

[ii]The full debate can be found at www.tandfonline.com/toc/tsrm20/23/5?nav=tocList

a methodological problem than that of measuring attributes that have several categories, such as ethnicity. The latter is particularly difficult, because although ethnicity is an attribute, ethnic identity is subjectively held, though ethnic relations are often objectively experienced, by individuals, though racism. Nevertheless, two individuals with the same heritage background may regard themselves as belonging to different ethnic groups (Williams & Husk, 2013).

Part of this problem is the number of available ethnic categories available to a respondent. For the researcher, there is a methodological/sociological trade-off. A small number of categories are easier to analyse because they produce larger cell sizes, but they are less valid measures of ethnicity, and a large number of categories, which produces better validity, but small cell sizes,[iii] may not be statistically significant, and this will have consequences for the analysis (Williams & Husk, 2013).

What we research, what we measure and how we measure it are inevitably socially situated, but this is actually true also of the statistics we use for analysis. Though it is true – and this is actually very important – that a particular statistical or analysis procedure is *as used* socially 'neutral', which analyses and statistical procedures *we choose* are socially situated. In some instances, different statistical procedures will produce the same outcomes in the same data set (a form of triangulation), regardless of the social motivation of the research or questions arising. On other occasions, the choice of which procedure to adopt can be a question of political motivation. Take the case of odds ratios[iv] in a logit model (see Volume 8), for example, as in the case of Herrnstein and Murray's *The Bell Curve* (see methodological critique of this by Drew et al., 1995). What is much more common are social trends in the choice of types of analyses, or statistical procedures. For example, mathematical statisticians and decision analysts have long favoured Bayesian methods of statistical inference, but only very recently have they been more widely adopted in other social science disciplines. Structural equation modelling (see Volume 10), once mainly used by psychologists and then economists, is now widely used, whereas discriminant function analysis (assigning individuals to outcome classes on the basis of a set of predictor variables), popular

---

[iii]Suppose you have a cross-tabulation of self-reported health and ethnicity. You have conducted this analysis to see whether different ethnic groups report health differently. Now, further suppose that there are very few people in one ethnic group, so that one 'cell' in your table is very small. Other cells will have (say) hundreds of respondents, but one cell has four respondents. The problems are this. That cell may be too small for any statistical test of association to be meaningful or 'statistically significant' (a concept you will encounter in Volumes 2 and 3). Secondly, it might be possible to discover the identity of those respondents, because there are so few of them. We discuss this later.

[iv]An 'odds ratio' is the ratio of one odds to another. The size of any relationship is measured by the difference (in either direction) from 1.0. An odds ratio less than 1.0 indicates an inverse or negative relation. An odds ratio greater than 1.0 indicates a direct or positive relationship.

some years ago, is little used. Factor analysis (now a component of structural equation modelling known as a 'measurement model') is being eclipsed by propensity score matching (creating comparison groups on the basis of multivariate profiles), and cluster analysis (defining homogeneous groups of individuals on the basis of a measure of 'closeness', e.g. as used in symptom profiling) is undergoing something of a revival! We hesitate to call these fashions; no doubt the practitioners of the currently popular methods (most recently, e.g., machine learning and neural networks) would claim that these methods are more fit for purpose than those they superseded, but equally social processes are at work in supervisor–student relations, the number and quality of training courses and/or other resources available.

A question of values

So far in this chapter we have painted a picture of quantitative methods as hugely influenced and shaped by non-methodological social processes and influences. If this argument holds (at least intuitively), how can we be good scientists? Particularly, how can we be objective scientists?

The decision to fund X or Y, to ask a particular question and not another, to structure questions in one way rather than another or to opt to use one type of analysis rather than another are a matter of values. Values are so often presented as only consisting of moral values, but they are more complex than that, and it is perhaps helpful to think of values as existing along a continuum. Let us think first of those with the least social content – those of numeric values – the mathematics that underlie our statistics. These are grounded in probability and at first sight have no social content, but wait! There are different interpretations of probability, each fulfilling the axioms of probability theory, for example, the frequency interpretation of probability (that underpins survey research), the propensity interpretation of probability (which underlies certain statistical procedures) and the 'subjective', or Bayesian, interpretation (Gillies, 2000). That the first of these has dominated social science is the result of particular events in the history of statistics, but it could have been otherwise.

Next in the value continuum might be the methodological values that lead to choices about whether to conduct primary research, or use secondary analysis, the type of survey used (e.g. self-completion or interview schedule) and the choice of analysis strategy (as mentioned in Chapter 7), as outlined above. These decisions may themselves rest on resource decisions, such as time, money or expertise (see Chapter 4).

Finally, there are the research questions that are asked and the political values that underwrite the funding regimes and research topics that are investigated.

Values in social research are not discrete, they are actually continuous, and if you think about the above examples, it is possible to imagine how one set of values shades into another. One obvious conclusion of this is that claims to value freedom are both a performative contradiction (because the claim itself is a value) and that moral values (what is usually meant by value freedom) are not so easily separated from other values.

Objectivity as socially situated

This then brings us to the matter of **objectivity**. For the proponents and opponents of value freedom, objectivity is seen as the attempt to be value free in social research (Williams, 2006). But value freedom and objectivity are not the same thing. The former is not possible, the latter is.

The latter is possible if we treat it as a value in itself. This in turn has important implications for how we think of the methodology, politics and ethics of social research.

Science itself is built on values, and indeed if those values had not come to the fore during its history, then there would be no science as we know it. Values such as parsimony (https://effectiviology.com/parsimony), consistency, rationality, truth and objectivity are at the basis of scientific method, in natural and social science. Some of these values, such as parsimony (see Nolan, 1997) and truth, transcend time and place, but objectivity is situated in time and place, but it also has generic characteristics than can transcend time and place (Newton-Smith, 1981).

Objectivity has been defined in many different ways (see Janack, 2002), but what most definitions have in common is a desire to provide a historically and socially neutral term. But, the problem with this is that it ignores the context in which objectivity operates. All research has purpose, and this seems to be a necessary (if trivial) condition. Thus, we might think of objectivity starting from a particular purpose, which will determine which questions or methods are appropriate. A second characteristic of investigation is that scientists treat phenomena as if they are real (and consequently have causal consequences). Those causal consequences, particularly in the social world, will depend on the question asked in the first place, so purpose and phenomena are linked. Finally, the search for truth, where truth is in agreement with reality, is a goal which transcends any context, but its search is shaped by that context (Williams, 2006).

A more sociological understanding of objectivity is that it is a value which itself transcends time and place but operates in the context of time and place. If an investigative priority is the social conditions and determinants of health and illness, then this will lead to questions and methods appropriate to its investigation. Had the priority been environmental sustainability, then these are likely to be different. So though we begin with values and values suffuse the whole investigative process (Longino, 1990), within these objectivity remains possible and necessary for good science. This was neatly summed up by Alvin Gouldner (1973):

> The physician is not necessarily less objective because he has made a partisan commitment to his patient and against the germ. The physician's objectivity is in some measure vouchsafed because he has committed himself to a specific value: health. (p. 58)

The politics of social research

If objectivity is socially situated and methodological choices are taken within the context of what is researched, does this mean that, like taxis at the rank, researchers are available to research anything that is the political choice of those who command the resources that make one research topic possible to research and another not so? Should researchers absolve themselves of any moral qualms about what they research as long as they assiduously search for the truth and uphold the other kinds of scientific values we indicated above? Does it follow from this that objectivity could even operate within a research agenda that began from questionable moral assumptions?

This is complicated, because one person's questionable moral assumption is another's moral good. Added to this are the power relations that exist in the research process. We have used the term *researchers* in a rather simple way that blurs the distinction between seniority, in particular, and other nuanced differences such as gender and ethnicity. Most of the contributors to the volumes in this Kit are 'tenured' professors and are to some extent in a position to choose, on political, moral and methodological grounds, which research they will pursue, though they too must pursue funding opportunities, consultancies and so on, as conditions of employment. In other words, they are free, though not entirely free, to exercise their choices as citizens to inform the research they do as scientists. But the early-career researcher, fresh from their PhD and possibly with a young family to support has fewer choices and may feel compromised into doing research that, in other circumstances, they would not undertake.

In Western countries, these political choices are rarely to be made on the basis of accepting questionable moral values. Funded research rarely begins from a basis of racism, sexism or homophobia. Things are much more nuanced than that, and actually, the problem often lies with *not* being able to research those topics that one, as a researcher, feels to be important. It is a politics of omission, rather than commission, much of the time. The sifting often begins at the level of PhD research. Several candidates may apply to study for a PhD at any given university and may each be as qualified and motivated as the other. Methodologically their proposals may be equally sound, but often the successful candidates will be those who propose topics that are relevant to research programmes currently in favour. Indeed, many research programmes will build PhD research into their work, and a candidate must choose (or not) to apply to research that topic.

Occasionally, it is not the topic itself that is politically controversial, but where the funding for it comes from. There is, for example, a history (particularly in the USA) of the military funding social research for its own ends, some of which have been seen as highly questionable by social scientists (Horowitz, 1967). Yet, even some military-funded and motivated research can yield unexpected insights, such as that of the sociologist Samuel Stouffer (Stouffer, 1949), who conducted organisational research with the US army, just after World War II, that had profound effects on our understanding of the structure of organisations more generally.

Sometimes questionable research with overt political agendas produces findings that are arrived at through a flawed methodological process or interpretation/selection of the results.

A good example of this and one quite controversial at the time was Peter Saunders's (1990) research of home ownership. Saunders, unusually amongst sociologists, is on the political 'right', and he claimed that his work was intended to confront the left academic orthodoxy (p. 7). He was primarily interested in the consequences of the growth of home ownership on individuals and British society more generally. His initial motivation and his conclusion was that this is overall a good thing.

His research was an interview-based survey with members of 450 households (522 individuals) living in three towns and in three types of housing, all at the lower end of the market and characterised by a preponderance of recent buyers, though around a third of the sample were council (public housing) tenants. His conclusions supported his initial views about the benefits of home ownership, specifically a greater likelihood to participate in local organisations and have a greater social engagement generally, that home ownership generates greater ontological security and, importantly, that homeowners have made substantial gains from buying property and it will have major consequences for the distribution of wealth and life chances in Britain. Indeed, he concluded, home ownership should be further encouraged to prevent non-owners from slipping into a marginalised underclass. Only through home ownership can such groups escape state dependency and become active citizens participating in the market.

Fiona Devine and Sue Heath (1999) presented a number of criticisms of Saunders's (1990) research: some are methodological and others are that he makes unsubstantiated claims from the data to support his position. The former criticisms include the choice of three industrial towns, rather than a national sample. These towns are almost certainly not typical, and generalisations to Britain as a whole are unwarranted.

Second, the sample size is too small. This presents problems of cell sizes (see above) in the multivariate analysis and reduces the scope to examine the 'association between several variables at once' and 'estimates from sample statistics to population parameters are imprecise', and apparently, substantial differences between groups in the sample might not signal real differences across the population (Devine & Heath, 1999, p. 95). Third, non-response was high, and in some groups possibly influenced findings.

The second kind of criticism concerns Saunders's overall claims, particularly in respect of the equity advantages gained by the home owners. These were far from equally distributed across classes, and from Saunders's data it is clear that the middle classes benefited disproportionately. Devine and Heath (1999) also draw attention to analyses that were not made/presented but should have been. What were the differences between home owners and tenants in respect of 'sex, age, ethnicity, employment status and occupational class to get a feel for the two categories of people whose attitudes and behaviour Saunders subsequently compares and contrasts' (p. 101).

In some ways, Saunders (1990) was an easy target, because, unlike other researchers, he was transparent about his methods, but though he began from an ideological position, the weakness of his methods and the overclaiming that followed undermined his initial position. Moreover, what is especially interesting about this historical example is that many now believe that the expansion of home ownership, at the expense of public housing, severely undermined social solidarity (Jacobs et al., 2003); thus, more contemporary research begins from quite different ideological premises.

However, whilst ideology is inevitably in the background and often the motivation for our theories, it does not have to be a determinant of our methods and results. A search for the truth would commit us to most effective methods to test our theories. In the Saunders (1990) case, either his research lacked methodological competence (unlikely in such an experienced researcher) or what he wanted to find to support his theoretical conjecture led him to the methods he used. Other more rigorous methods, particularly in respect of sampling, would have generated different results.

Ethics in a social context

One can perhaps view the search for truth as the key ethic of science, but in social science, as we have indicated, this will inevitably be in a social context. Yet, beyond complex ideological considerations, the ethics of what we should and shouldn't research often enjoy a widespread consensus in the research community. For example, research for, or funded by, the tobacco or arms industry is seen as unethical by most researchers. Research with vulnerable adults and with children, though not impossible, is usually subject to a number of constraints intended to protect these groups.

Many professional bodies (e.g. the Social Research Association, in the UK, The British Sociological Association and the American Psychological Association) publish ethical guidelines for research that they expect their members to adhere to. Although there is little or no discussion of prior motivations or ideological agendas, these guidelines often have a commonality in respect of the key ethical tenets. Versions of these, in turn, often form the basis of university ethical policies. In these, the broader political and ideological issues we have described above are often left implicit, and the ethical concerns are principally about respondents.

Most ethical codes of conduct outline four key ethical principles in respect of the researcher–respondent/participant relationship.

The avoidance of harm: what effects will the research have on others?

No research act is without some social consequences, though mostly these are entirely benign. However, the literature in psychology, anthropology and sociology is replete with examples of research that had well-intended aims having serious effects on participants, or others, who happened to be in the vicinity. For survey researchers, adverse effects are rare but are not absent. In 1997, researchers at the Universities of Wolverhampton and Birmingham were forced to abandon a survey researching post-traumatic stress disorder. The self-completion questionnaire was sent to a sample of residents of Dunblane, where a number of children had been shot in the local school some months before.[v] The researchers withdrew the questionnaire and apologised.

More mundanely, in designing one's questionnaire, careful consideration should be given to the effects particular questions might have on certain groups. For example, sensitivity to religious beliefs and practices or questions that are of a very personal nature.

But the researcher's duty does not finish in the ethical design and execution of research. What will the findings be used for and could they be misused? Obviously, researchers are powerless to stop others taking their findings out of context, or deliberately misinterpreting or misrepresenting them. If the sponsors of one's research have a particular ideological goal, then it should not surprise us if they then use the findings to further that goal. But, this aside, misinterpretation or misrepresentation can be mitigated to an extent by very clear presentation of findings and where perhaps statistical uncertainty, for example, is present, then an honest appraisal of the findings is a much safer strategy than overclaiming!

---

[v]Reported in the *Guardian* newspaper 15 January 1997.

The avoidance of deception

Under what circumstances is it acceptable for a researcher to deceive? There is an important methodological point that because researchers are scientists, then inevitably their knowledge of the area of investigation will be greater than that of the lay person. In most surveys, for example, there would not be time or would respondents usually welcome a detailed explanation of what the survey was about. Yet, in most cases, a written or spoken introduction (depending on the mode of data collection) explaining what the research is about is usual and right and proper. This can be done usually in a few sentences, and these days it is not uncommon for further details to be available on a website. Obviously, within the survey, strategies to test knowledge, beliefs and attitudes, perhaps through items in scales (as illustrated in Chapter 7 regarding the assessment of cognitive function and well-being), are a mild form of deception, but at this level, providing this does not lead to psychological harm, then it is legitimate.

The right to privacy

In quantitative research, the issue of privacy is primarily one of which data can be collected and who has access to it, at the time of the research and later. Respondents' right to privacy is, to some extent, enshrined in laws such as the Data Protection Act in the UK, for example, or the Freedom of Information Act in the USA.

So what kinds of issues can arise? The one that has long been present is that of anonymity. Most social research surveys will be prefaced or ended by a guarantee of anonymity – that the data collected will only be used for statistical purposes and respondents will not be identified. Most universities have policies regarding the storage and access to subsequent data that will uphold such declarations.

Privacy is more likely to be violated by accident than design, particularly in surveys. Survey data are usually anonymised. This means that respondents are not anonymous, but their identity cannot be discerned from the output from analyses. Unfortunately, small cell sizes have the potential to reveal a person's identity. This is primarily a problem in cross-tabulations, with a third or more control variables – for example, rather than have a simple cross-tabulation for ethnicity and self-reported health for the whole sample, the relationship you might want to examine is the relationship between biological sex and/or state or county of residence and a dependent variable with several categories. One of us (Malcolm) conducted research on living alone, using the UK *Office for National Statistics Longitudinal Study*, for England and Wales (Ware et al., 2007). This is a longitudinally linked sample of census records with 500,000 cases! Possibly one of the largest data sets available in the world.

A 12-category household structure variable was derived, but when this was used in cross-tabulations that had previously selected two other variables, one of the cells in the table actually had less than five people in it!

Government surveys and censuses often go to great trouble to anonymise records (Dale & Marsh, 1993, pp. 119–125), and sometimes they insist on the inspection of any output prior to publication. Data presented in cross-tabulations may be subject to the 'suppression' of cells with a count of less than five, such as that indicated above. This is possibly of dubious value, because it is fairly easy to calculate the number in the cell from the row and column counts.

However, it is likely to be a smaller-scale survey where this becomes an important issue where the total sample size (N) is just a few hundred cases. What might make a difference here is the specificity of the community research, either its geographical location or a community of interest. For example, research on sufferers (or carers of) a rare disease may have used the database of a support group to obtain the sample, and consequently the subsequent identification of members of that group would not be difficult for a third party.

The principle of informed consent

Informed consent and the avoidance of deception are somewhat linked, though as with the former this does not imply that respondents should have a detailed knowledge of the research. They should, however, know enough of the purpose of the research and what happens to their data, before they agree to participate. In large-scale 'curated' surveys, such as *Understanding Society*, the data will be analysed mostly as a secondary resource for many purposes, unlike, for example, a one-off cross-sectional survey about attitudes to the building of a new airport runway. Thus, the storage of data, rules of disclosure, anonymity and secure access by only approved persons become very important issues, and in effect, respondents are placing trust in researchers to get these things right. This has become an even more crucial and controversial issue in recent years, when the merging of data sets, or the linking of individual survey data to the same individual's record in administrative data (or parts thereof), became technically possible (see Calderwood & Lessof, 2009; Meyer & Mittag, 2019). Similarly, some cohort studies (such as the UK *Millennium Cohort Study*) collect biological and genetic samples (Joshi & Fitzsimmons, 2016).

Sometimes, again particularly when reanalysing data or repurposing administrative data for other research, individual consent is not always possible. The UK Data Service provide some specific guidelines on this, so that if research without informed consent is to be conducted,

- there must be clear value and benefit from doing the research,
- no alternative research design can achieve the same result – that is, the deception or lack of consent is essential and
- there is no or very minimal risk of harm to participants.

UK Data Service (www.ukdataservice.ac.uk/manage-data/legal-ethical/consent-data-sharing/surveys) provide detailed and useful information and resources on their website that might be used across a range of quantitative research, including consent forms and consent statements. It is also worth consulting a seminal article on the codification of statistical ethics by (the late) Roger Jowell (1986; former Director of the National Centre for Social Research and the European Social Survey).

How do we decide on the nature/quality of evidence from other studies?

This is where ethics and literature review connect! Poor research will cherry-pick earlier research to find that which is conducive to its theoretical position, or if opposed can easily be shown to be poor or misconceived. Good research will sift through the previous research and look for that which was the most thorough and methodologically robust. In quantitative research, this would include a large enough and representative sample, a good-quality data collection instrument (e.g. a questionnaire) that had been thoroughly piloted, administered and tested. There may not be one form of analysis that is appropriate, but nevertheless it is possible to scrutinise analyses for appropriateness. Were the correct dependent variables and control variables chosen and statistical analysis and conclusions supported by the data? Were the analyses statistically significant? If multivariate analyses were used, were things like odds ratios or goodness of fit (a family of various measures used to assess how close your observed [raw] data are to values predicted by an underlying statistical model or procedure) interpreted correctly? More difficult to call, were the analyses 'parsimonious' or were extremely elaborate methods used and results selectively chosen? In other words, did the researchers torture the data to get their results!

Assessing the **research quality** of the work of others can make us better researchers, because it alerts us to the political and methodological basis of the research, helping us to avoid the pitfalls that such an assessment uncovers. But also an assessment of research, during a literature review, can help you make decisions about citation, or replication of elements of that research, say its sample strategy, questionnaire or analyses. Below is a checklist of some of the things to look out for in the research of others.

Box 8.1: A Research Quality Checklist

✓ Who funded the research and what was the origin of the research questions?
✓ What might have been counterfactual questions? In other words, was the research setting out to prove a position or phenomenon?
✓ Who would be the beneficiaries of the research?
✓ Was the conduct of the fieldwork ethical?
✓ Did the sampling strategy adequately reflect the population composition?
✓ What kind of survey was conducted (e.g. face to face, online or telephone)?
✓ What questionnaire piloting was conducted?
✓ Are the questions reliable and valid?
✓ Are important questions missing?
✓ What checks on data quality were conducted?
✓ What was the level and nature of non-response?
✓ What is the extent of item non-response, and are there any patterns in this?
✓ Were strategies such as weighting or imputation used?
✓ Was the analysis strategy justified, by the researchers, and was it appropriate?
✓ Do the analyses support any conclusions drawn?

Except in large national studies, of the kind mentioned above, it would be hard to answer all of the questions above, in respect of most studies. Data archives will often require some of this information, but journal articles themselves will rarely provide it, on the practical grounds of space, but they may provide a link to supplementary information about the data, research strategy, additional analyses and checks, as well as the data source itself.[vi]

In recent years, there have been a number of initiatives to make visible these kinds of things. Much of these efforts are part of the Open Science Movement. This is not a single organisation, but cumulative efforts to make scientific research accessible, not just to other scientists but also to the public generally. What the principles of the movement are and its nature are the subject of debate (Fecher & Friesike, 2014), and different positions advocate different priorities, such as open data, knowledge creation, measurement, governance and so on. Although the movement has gained momentum, in recent years, the sentiment toward openness in science goes back much further. In the last century, Karl Popper (1966) saw open science as the

---

[vi]Many journals now require that data and instruments from research, and referred to in academic articles, are also made accessible to the reader. In practice, this may consist of anonymised data files, codebooks and questionnaires.

cornerstone of an open society, one that develops through testing and problem solving. Helen Longino (1990), whose work was grounded in feminist empiricism, saw the scientific community as the arbiter of truth. Indeed, what we describe as 'situated objectivity' also requires transparency of intention, data and methods.

What does this mean in practice for quantitative researchers? The move to open access, for published findings, has gained particular momentum. Traditionally, academic publishing in journals required a subscription to the journal, or, more commonly nowadays, payment to view an article. But now there is pressure, particularly from funding councils, to make results accessible to all through 'Open Access'. In practice, this means that the researcher, or their organisation, pays the publishing fee so that the reader can simply download the paper.

Conclusion

All science has a social context. Science itself is a social product, albeit one whose results can transcend particular social contexts. For social science research, this is even more of a challenge, because researchers are part of the social context they are researching. That is, the questions asked mostly come from the society in which the researcher is a social actor and the questions asked inevitably have a political or ideological origin. This does not mean objectivity is not possible, but objectivity is a social value that exists in context but can transcend that context through good scientific method. Good science should also be open to scrutiny, and the careful examination of how other researchers go through their data and reached their conclusions is a valuable part of the process of learning to be a social researcher.

For social researchers, the 'materials' of their science are people themselves, and this places limits on what kind of research can be done and how it can be done. The ethics of social research are both broad and narrow. Broad in the sense that society and the community of social scientists will set ethical limits on what kind of research can be conducted and things like how it is funded and who will benefit from it. And narrow in the sense that at the level of data gathering the data comes from individuals, who are seen to have rights over their own data.

Chapter Summary

- No research takes place in a moral or political vacuum; moreover, in our view, there is no such thing as value-free research. These things are connected, and in this chapter we discuss three important issues: firstly, we examine some of the issues in the context of social research, such as policy priorities and funding regimes.

- Secondly, the ways in which research, though it must begin from a value position, can nevertheless be objective. This then has implications for research ethics and the role of the researcher in conducting ethical and responsible research.
- Finally, in this chapter, we offer some brief advice on assessing research quality.

Further Reading

Letherby, G., Scott, J., & Williams, M. (2013). *Objectivity and subjectivity in social research*. Sage.

Much of the writing on objectivity and subjectivity is somewhat simplistic, but if you want to look at a more nuanced approach – that is a debate between three similar but differing perspectives – you may wish to read the above.

Hammersley, M. (1995). *The politics of social research*. Sage.

Although many textbooks will discuss the ethics of research, in respect of participants, few discuss in detail the politics of research. And yet social research has become politicised. Martyn Hammersley asks must we choose between this and 'value freedom'?

9

CONCLUSION AND FUTURE DIRECTIONS

Congratulations, you have reached a point of departure! The volumes that follow will in this *SAGE Quantitative Research Kit* build upon the foundations laid in this volume so that you can begin to 'deepen' your knowledge and understanding of the process of being a quantitative social researcher. Recap upon what you have acquired in earlier chapters. In Chapter 1, we set the scene: social research is a broad church wherein research problems range from the straightforward to the complex just like the tools (techniques) we bring to bear in order to come up with plausible evidence. Our choice of tool will be informed by methodological reasoning. It's tempting to think that what distinguishes quantitative and qualitative research is the difference between numbers and words but that would miss a lot of the subtleties of doing research. The numbers we generate or use in quantitative research don't just appear, they are the result of carefully crafted literature reviews, decisions about whether or not to undertake primary or secondary research, how to collect data and how to codify responses. On their own, numbers are identifiable labels without meaning until the researcher brings further information along in order to situate the various numbers as values of defined variables. In the application of techniques to draw out patterns, relationships and summaries, we produce visual displays and subsequent 'numbers' that have a special role to play as statistics. This phase of analysis, involving both description and explanation and possibly to-ing and fro-ing from simple description to complex analysis, becomes the 'seedcorn' of our enterprise whereupon the written interpretation of your findings becomes all important. You arrive at a narrative expressed in words, supported by a coherent argument, based upon your data analysis. Once your written account receives external approval, the publication of a dissertation report, a thesis, a pre-print or possibly as a peer-reviewed journal article, you begin to lose control over its influence. This is the point at which the knowledge you have created begins to become wisdom. At the core of your quantitative research is description and inference, which have the potential to lead to causal explanation and prediction. There are no panaceas about how to do quantitative research. It's important to feel confident about your science, the basis of your research questions, your choice of methodology and your readiness to both defend your decisions to do things in a certain way and support the implications of your interpretations with evidence.

The following 10 volumes build upon the fundamental aspects of design, execution and analysis of quantitative research. In particular, the next six volumes focus on the basics of observation and preliminary analysis. Assuming that your prior knowledge begins with a final-year social science view of social research, which includes more than an interest in data handling and analysis, these early volumes will deepen your practical knowledge of doing research. Volumes 7 through 10 represent a statistical 'step up', and finally, Volume 11 seizes a new reality in a world where data is 'big' but not necessarily collected under the rigours of scientific method. Gaining knowledge from such sources presents new challenges for the data analyst. What follows is a summary description of how each chapter in this volume serves as a 'spring board' for later volumes, although not all chapters directly to a particular volume. Some stand alone, while others feed into more than one volume. In previous chapters, we have already done some of this signposting, but we are now bringing things together as a 'railroad map' for the rest of your journey. The chapter concludes with a formal description of each volume in the Kit.

We hope that Chapter 2 appealed to those of you who appreciate the advantages of multidisciplinary research, in that as quantitative researchers we are typically students of a problem rather than a discipline. We convert problems into research questions typically expressed as hypotheses, which can be tested empirically. However, our quest is not simply one of gathering empirical evidence. It is important to remember that our research is not solely 'problem orientated'. Theory has an important role to play in the formulation of our research strategy, not so much as 'grand theory' but theory with testable consequences. We go on to distinguish between variables and cases as we descend the ladder of abstraction. In quantitative research, variables are ubiquitous, but whilst they 'pop' up all the time they can have a special status as predictor, independent, outcome, dependent, confounder, mediator or moderator, whereas a case is typically an individual made up of operationalisable variables! Generally speaking, a case is your unit of analysis, which could be a school or a neighbourhood, themselves aggregates of individuals. In lots of ways, Chapter 2 puts down a foundation for the language of research in all of the illustrations that follow. Beyond the operationalisation of research questions, we have to consider the extent to which your research investigation is descriptive or explanatory or a combination of both. In particular, Volume 2 by Julie Scott Jones and John Goldring provides a repertoire of descriptive statistics to help you get to know your data source, and Volume 3 by John MacInnes develops what is meant by statistical inference and the application of probability. Chapter 2 suggests that explanation implies causality, and we learn that causality is a word that can mean different things to different researchers. We don't hide from this realisation as you will contrast between some of the views presented in this volume and Matthew McBee's introduction to causal analysis in Volume 10.

If it were physically possible to place two chapters in parallel, Chapter 3 on literature reviews and meta-analyses would sit alongside Chapter 2 because conducting a literature review and refining your research question are iterative or complementary activities. Often, it feels like a literature review is never finished as there will be inevitable gaps in your reviewing and new research findings emerge as you are developing your own agenda. In many ways, this chapter stands alone as regards not having a specific volume to underpin. But that doesn't diminish its value or importance, and we would emphasise that the remainder of the activities discussed in this volume – from research design, sampling plan, methods of data collection, the ethical conduct of research and devising analysis plans – can all be enhanced by effective reviewing of the research literature and so too are the volumes which enlarge upon these dimensions, namely, Volume 4 on 'Survey Research and Sampling' by Jan Eichhorn, Volume 5 on 'Archival and Secondary Data Analysis' by Tarani Chandola and Cara Booker and Volume 6 on 'Experimental Designs' by Barak Ariel, Matthew Bland and Alex Sutherland. Indeed, acquiring competence in the conduct of systematic reviews and meta-analysis is a desirable tool to add to your skill set at some point.

Chapter 4 extends the consideration of description and explanation into causal analysis and meaning and their relationship to theory into de Vaus's four principle designs for research: (1) the cross-sectional, (2) the case study, (3) the experimental and (4) the longitudinal designs each of which find a way into various volumes. The design of cross-sectional studies is covered in Volume 4, their use as secondary sources in Volume 5 and the necessary handling and inference for these studies in Volumes 2 and 3. Case studies may well complement a cross-sectional design as an in-depth analysis of many variables within a case (however, defined). In your reading of the literature, you must be ready to encounter these designs and remember that they are not always mutually exclusive. Moving on to consider experimental designs, which is at the heart of quantitative researcher's endeavour to capture causality and owe their origins to the physical sciences, Volume 6 by Barak Ariel and his colleagues deepens the account of experimentation and provides a rich selection of informative examples which will appeal to readers who are interested in criminology. Today, evidence-based research and the evaluation of policy interventions have embraced the RCT; however, whilst the theory of randomisation is fundamental in our argument to establish cause and effect, it is often difficult to implement in practice with human populations. We introduce a longitudinal study in Chapter 7 and subsequently in Volumes 3, 5 and 9. Chapter 4 concludes with the important consideration of resources in the broadest sense of time, effort, human resources, the use of available data and computer power. Put formally, the practice planning and budgeting is another competence that you will need to develop.

Chapter 5 on sampling anticipates Volume 4 by Jan Eichhorn by starting out with some of the basics, including arithmetic, probability and the various ways and means of designing a sample sometimes avoiding the 'gold standard' of having an 'all singing all dancing' probability sample. Whether or not you embark on designing a survey or using an existing cross-sectional or longitudinal survey, you will need to be able to critically develop and evaluate sampling strategies. Chapter 6 is a natural extension of Chapter 5 and underpins Volume 4 in terms of designing survey questionnaires, the importance of measurement and evaluation of several questions or items used to measure an underlying concept (scaling). This takes us into a consideration of key methodological tools in the assessment of survey questionnaires – namely, definitions of reliability and validity. Questionnaire evaluation concerns the internal properties of measures, whereas the quality of the sampling strategy is a permit to generalise.

Chapter 7 is the first chapter to expose the reader to the delights of using software via the familiar work horse SPSS, in the context of a case study on well-being of 50-year-olds on the cusp of the third age. Here, we introduce the reader to real data in order to prepare for the experience of having some insight about the need to check and manipulate data prior to any analysis. The case study draws upon variables which capture aspects of childhood and adolescence to illustrate the use of a longitudinal birth cohort study. In this way, we can appreciate the fact that what might be thought of as a cross-sectional variable like 'well-being' carries not only influences in the present but also in the past. As you begin to read Volumes 7 and 8 by Peter Martin and beyond, you will be introduced to analytical tools (namely, multiple regression) which provide the capacity to predict well-being on the basis of childhood and adolescent variables. Volume 5 also continues with the use of available data, both survey and administrative, and extends the application of software to include STATA and SAS commands.

Quantitative research doesn't exist in a vacuum. All social research is located in a social world which defines our existence, interests, aspirations and motivation to be researchers. Chapter 8 provides an account of the tension that arises once we recognise that the context in which we carry out research may challenge our claims to be objective. Under our efforts to engage in 'value-free' research, objectivity is best seen as a value alongside truth, rationality, parsimony and consistency, and together, these values inform our choices in research, whether it be what we choose to investigate and how we choose to collect and analyse information. What gets on to the research agenda and what gets funded also has to be seen in a political context where priorities are moulded into shape. Being aware of these social and political influences should not dissuade us from actually embarking upon research but instead to do so in an ethical manner. What emerges from this chapter is a framework that enables you to critically evaluate the quality of the research you digest as part of your literature and the degree of self-evaluation of your own endeavours. To that extent the chapter underpins all volumes that draw upon the work of others (Volume 5) and empowers you to make the best use of your data (Volumes 7, 8, 9 and 10). Remember also to examine the choice of statistical methodology in context.

Statistics lie at the heart of quantitative research; they are the means through which we can express how we can infer from samples to populations and how we might show relationships between variables. Most of the volumes in the Kit are concerned with forms of analysis, and these utilise statistics. The way in which the Kit unfolds is like a slow train moving out of the platform (Volume) 1. First, demonstrating how simple descriptives help you explore your data in Volume 2, the business of making generalisable statements or testing hypotheses in Volume 3, the art of sampling in Volume 4 and the use of secondary data in Volume 5. The fifth volume recognises that an increasing amount of social research is conducted on previously gathered data. These data might be from large-scale one–off surveys, 'panel studies' of the same people at regular intervals or official statistics, such as census data. These data sets provide opportunities to analyse data from many thousands of people. In Volume 7, Peter Martin introduces the basic ideas which define statistical modelling where we encounter prediction in the form of multiple regression. Imagine at this juncture the train sighs and waits at a major interchange before climbing out of the world of doing social research into a world where the gradient steadily increases and reveals deeper forests of knowledge which coexist alongside the rail tracks as points of new discovery. Volume 8 expands the coverage of regression modelling to properly account for measures which are no longer assumed to be continuous, where outcomes may be categorical (binary and more) or counts. Stopping at a recently modernised station (Volume 9), D. Betsy McCoach and Dakota W. Cintron invite you to learn more about models which enable you to take proper account of hierarchical or clustered data (aka hierarchical linear modelling or multilevel modelling) and structural equation modelling. The latter facilitates an accommodation of both measurement models (operationalising concepts by means of multiple indicators or items) and their structural relationship between one another. Both of these methods build upon Peter Martin's earlier volumes and can be thought of as an extension of a regression framework. In Volume 10, Matthew McBee brings us back to the land of causality with many useful applications of R programming. At the final destination, the train plateau's, but there's no time to snooze and take in the scenery; in our final Volume, 11, Brian Castellani and Rajeev Rajaram put data mining before you in a world where data is generated as a result of the everyday business of life and not as science per se. New technologies, in recent years, have provided new opportunities to research enormous amounts of data harvested from everyday transactions and through the use of new communication methods, such as Twitter and Facebook. Their volume introduces a range of techniques for searching for meaning across large and complex data. What follows now is a brief formal description of each volume and then a lookup table (Table 9.1) which connects each chapter in this volume with later ones.

Box 9.1: Formal Description of Volumes 2 Through 11

In *Volume 2*, Julie Scott Jones and John Goldring provide an accessible introduction to the basics of how we can describe data and how we might begin to explore it. As in the previous volume, real examples are used to show how we can 'tell stories with data'.

Volume 3, by John MacInnes, introduces some of the most important concepts in data analysis that inform the later more statistical volumes: with the basic question of what is meant by probability in its 'objective' and 'subjective' forms? How does probabilistic thinking translate into testable statistical hypotheses? How do we infer from our data and how do we infer from observed effects to causality? Finally, he emphasises the importance of replication in social research.

Volume 4, by Jan Eichhorn, is concerned with surveys and sampling. Through a number of illustrative case studies and examples, it explains the theory and practice of sampling, questionnaire design and how to pilot questionnaires.

In *Volume 5*, Tarani Chandola and Cara Booker describe what is meant by secondary and archival research, its advantages and disadvantages and how to make choices about the data sets that might be used. They take us on a journey from these initial choices – how ideas can be translated into research questions, how variables in the data might be selected and manipulated, and how data might be described and presented.

Volume 6, by Barak Ariel, Matthew Bland and Alex Sutherland, provides a detailed description of randomised controlled trials and other approaches to experimentation, largely in the context of criminology. They carefully discuss the advantages and disadvantages of these approaches and provide practical guidance on how to design and conduct experiments.

Volume 7, by Peter Martin, is the first of two volumes which introduce the reader to statistical modelling. The whole approach rests on encouraging the reader to develop a 'modelling brain' and view the choice of a statistical model as being a quest for what technique is best suited for the task at hand rather than as a 'cookbook' recipe. What Peter achieves begins with a thorough introduction to the role and purpose of linear and multiple (linear) regression. The second volume expands the analysts' horizons to what plausible models there might be under different measurement assumptions.

In *Volume 8*, Peter Martin takes the reader beyond linear regression to develop modelling techniques which are appropriate for situations where the outcome variable is categorical or simply a count. In these non-linear applications, distributional assumptions are illuminated to build a framework for the general linear model.

Volume 9, by D. Betsy McCoach and Dakota W. Cintron, builds upon the regression modelling covered in Peter Martin's volumes to introduce two modern modelling techniques. Firstly, two-level multilevel modelling in which data are considered to be clustered or hierarchical (classic formulations in educational research where pupils are 'nested' within schools), and secondly, structural equation modelling which combines measurement modelling and regression to define structural relationships both linear

(Continued)

and non-linear in the context of path analysis (the pictorial representation of statistical associations). These techniques are both extended and combined in the context of longitudinal analysis.

Volume 10, by Matthew McBee, takes the reader beyond formal descriptions of randomised controlled trials as the 'gold standard' for establishing causality to a series of statistical approaches with numerous illustrations which draw upon the use of R. The techniques considered and commonly applied in economics, epidemiology and political science no longer depend on randomisation. These include regression discontinuity design, propensity score matching, instrumentation and counterfactual analysis. As a means of selecting suitable control variables, the reader is introduced to the use of directed acyclic graphs.

In Volume 11, Brian Castellani and Rajeev Rajaram introduce the current 'hot topics' of social media research and data mining. We hear much of 'big data', but how can researchers analyse and manipulate it? This, as Castellani and Rajaram explain, requires a new approach to thinking about data – that of 'complexity', and in turn this leads us both to new methods of analysis and creative ways of using the battery of existing methods.

We recommend that you work through Volumes 2 through 8 in a fairly linear fashion, and then, as your interest in statistical methods develops, select the remaining volumes in any order to suit your mood. The chapters in this volume may be revisited to kick-start your concentrated efforts, and the tables below might serve as a reminder as to how each chapter in this volume connects with Volumes 2 through 6 (Table 9.1) together with their call on software applications. Table 9.2 considers the more statistical volume to volume interactions (Volume 7 and beyond). These later volumes subsume the previous ones as summarised in Table 9.1.

Table 9.1 Chapter–volume interface

Chapter	Volume(s)	Software
1 A General Introduction to This Kit	Prerequisite for all	DNA
2 Starting With the Basics: From Research Problem to Variables	Prerequisite for all; highlights 3, 4, 7 and 9	Volume 9 is a forerunner into using R (lavaan) and/or MPlus
3 Literature Reviews and Meta-Analyses	Prerequisite for all; highlights 2, 3, 4 and 5	SPSS, STATA and SAS commands; be ready to decipher the use of statistics
4 Research Design and Research Resources	2, 5, 6 and 9; preparation and emphasis on fundamentals of design	DNA

Chapter	Volume(s)	Software
5 Sampling	2, 4 and 9	Excel (not explicit but a useful tool for handling sampling frames) and other aspects of use in Volume 2. Accounting for survey design in analysis under R, SPSS, STATA and SAS
6 Creating Data: An Introduction to Surveys and Questionnaires	4 and 5	SPSS (also Chapter 7, Volume 1)
7 Secondary Analysis and Data Manipulation	5	SPSS, STATA and SAS commands
8 The Social Context of Quantitative Research	All illustrations	

Table 9.2 Volume–volume interface (Volume 7 and beyond)

Volume	Volumes	Software
7 Linear Regression: An Introduction to Statistical Models	8, 9, 10 and 11	R illustrations
8 Regression Models for Categorical and Count Data	9, 10 and 11	R illustrations
9 Introduction to Modern Modelling Methods	7, 8 and 10	Signposting to R (lavaan) and MPlus
10 Statistical Approaches to Causal Analysis	7, 8 and 9	RStudio
11 Big Data Mining and Complexity	7, 8, 9 and 10	RStudio

Obviously, the above tables are only a guide. Just like the application of statistical methodology, your path does not have to be linear, and when you have digested the contents of this Kit, there will always be new research tools to acquire. Good luck with your reading and research.

GLOSSARY

Cases: Often in social science research a case typically represents an individual participant in a study. Not to be confused with case studies of a single person. However, cases need not be samples of individuals, they can include organisations like firms, schools, hospitals or buses. These groupings may be made up of individuals, but it is the unit as a whole that defines a case for which we have a specific interest (bankruptcy, school exclusions, bed capacity or keeping to the timetable). When defining a research question remember to be clear about what constitutes the unit of analysis (or case).

Data management: Includes the careful collection of numeric data from the classification of the original responses by measurement level, the construction of a coding frame (typically built into computer-assisted surveys), checking that individual variables are within the numeric range permitted and wherever appropriate checking the logic of the survey responses by means of consistency checks (arises when certain questions filter out subsamples). Prior to analysis this activity will also include an assessment of the extent of missing data. Preparing data for longitudinal analysis will involve merging sweeps or consecutive files of data. Having consistent case identification over time is a vital part of this process.

Ethics: This is a term used in several different, but overlapping, ways both in philosophy and in social research. In philosophy, it is the study of morality and often a search for universal forms of morality. In social research, ethical principles are embodied in codes of conduct aimed at protecting participants in research, but it can also refer to ethical principles in what kind of research is conducted and how/when it is reported (see also *The politics of social research*).

Hypothesis/es: Hypotheses and theories take the same logical form, if 'P then Q', but hypotheses play a more specific and closely defined form in social research. Firstly, they can be propositional statements, that if a set of conditions P hold, then Q will come about. This is usually referred to as a 'research hypothesis'. Secondly, though following the same logical form, they are used to test for the statistical significance of data. Statistical hypotheses incorporate probability into an expression that allows the researcher to accept or reject a hypothesis, thus emulating the laboratory procedure of the natural sciences whereby a hypothesis is either confirmed or falsified. Indeed, hypothesis testing has long been in favour in psychology, which is often laboratory based, but is used in quantitative social science, especially in experimental method (see also *Theory*).

Literature review: A survey and interpretation of previous research findings (the literature), aimed at providing an understanding what prior research was conducted, the way it was conducted and its findings. Literature reviews are usually an ongoing process in a research project, and it is normal to return to the literature, after the empirical work has been done, to help interpret and contextualise results.

Longitudinal data analysis: The analysis of repeat observations on individuals (cases) over time. The important distinction between longitudinal data of this type and repeat surveys which cover different samples of individuals over time known as continuous surveys is the unit of analysis – individuals or population aggregates.

Objectivity and subjectivity: Objectivity and subjectivity are sometimes seen as opposites, and the former is wrongly conflated with value freedom. Though social life is grounded in subjectivity and intersubjectivity, the goal of scientific social research is to conduct research that can transcend the investigator's own subjectivity. All research begins from values, moral or methodological, and these will shape research, they should not determine the findings (see also *The politics of social research*).

Probability sampling: Each individual has a known and calculable chance of selection unlike non-probability samples where this is not possible. In order to select a probability sample, it is necessary to obtain an up-to-date sampling frame (list) which covers the target population. The instances where probabilities of selection are not equal (disproportionate allocation) will require re-weighting at the analytical stage.

Questionnaire design: This is the process in which questions are devised with the aim of maximising validity and reliability and reducing non-response to the survey or the particular question. The questions mostly fall into three kinds: attributes, behaviour and attitudes/beliefs. The process of questionnaire design begins informally with concepts derived from research questions and is intended to then operationalise research hypotheses. This process is sometimes called 'descending the ladder of abstraction'. Specific questions are often pretested and the designed questionnaire is then piloted to reduce error and maximise validity and reliability.

Reliability: To what extent would our survey question provide similar responses if asked of the same respondents on another occasion? A measure can be reliable yet invalid. The concept of reliability is also pertinent in the case of using a group of items to assess an underlying concept (see *Scaling*) where our concern is with the internal consistency of the responses (high average inter-item correlation) often summarised by Cronbach's alpha (see also *Validity*).

Research design: This is the logic of inquiry that structures how the research is conducted. Following David de Vaus, this book proposes four kinds of design: experimental, longitudinal, cross-sectional and case study. Research designs do not imply specific methods, and different methods might be used in each of the designs. Although these four designs represent an 'ideal type', in practice a study might utilise a hybrid of these, for example, where case studies are embedded in a cross-sectional design (see also *Survey design*).

Research quality: Research quality is about maximising the methodological and ethical status of research. Research quality may be compromised by a number of diverse factors, including ideological positions, poor or insufficient resources, lack of researcher skills, poor research design, poor instrument (often questionnaire) design and incomplete or poor quality analyses.

Research questions: The problem to be investigated in a study stated in the form of a question, or questions. Research questions have an important role in focussing investigation, from gathering evidence to analysing data. Research questions usually precede a research hypothesis and, though less defined, will usually have explanatory content (see also *Hypothesis/es*).

Scaling: Refers to a methodology typically applied where the researcher is interested in measuring attitudes whereby a group of questions (items) are asked in order to assess the same underlying concept (e.g. well-being). The evaluation of a scale typically begins with an inspection of the inter-correlations between each pair of items in the scale and is often accompanied by multivariate analysis to confirm whether or not the survey items can be considered as measuring a single dimension. If so, researchers will add the numeric codes (adjusting for any reverse wording) to create a summative index or summary measure (in this case to indicate high or low expressions of well-being). The practice of scaling sits neatly under the measurement models used in structural equation modelling (see *The SAGE Quantitative ResearchKit*, Volume 9), where the survey items are observed indicators of an underlying unobserved concept.

Secondary data analysis: The analysis of available data, which can include text, artefacts, visual material, sound and numbers. In this series, the emphasis is on the statistical analysis of quantitative surveys.

Survey design: A generic term that captures all features of a survey, including the sample selection, the mode of data collection (face-to-face interviews, telephone, computer-assisted, online etc.) and the questionnaire (question order, wording, length), plans for follow-up calls or attempts to gain a response and sponsorship (academic, government, charity etc.; see also *Research design*).

Theory: Theories are all propositional statements of the form 'if *P* then *Q*'. Logically, they are equivalent to hypotheses, but theories are of quite different kinds. They may be informal 'folk theories', which differ little from everyday beliefs; they may be (in social science) 'grand theories', which offer an explanatory schema for a wide range of social phenomena; and they may be 'middle-range theories' (again in social science), which are close to those used by natural scientists and are testable statements which will explain a limited range of social phenomena, often within a particular socio-historical/cultural context (see also *Hypothesis/es*).

The politics of social research: Most research has political origins or consequences. This is not necessarily 'party political', or even ideological, but the consequence of choosing to research a particular topic and the social context of that topic. Similarly, once research is conducted, it may have political consequences and affect how public policy is created, interpreted, changed or discarded (see also *Ethics*).

Validity: Concerns the extent to which a measure actually measures what it sets out to achieve (e.g. psychiatric status). Does our measure represent the 'true' state (of belief, behaviour, circumstance) or not? The appraisal of a measure's validity will involve one or more of the following: face validity (do a group of experts agree about the face value of the survey questions?), content validity (does the measure cover all aspects of a concept, e.g. life satisfaction?), construct validity (the degree to which the measure accurately measures what it sets out to assess), concurrent validity (does theory or previous research suggest other key variables with which our measure is statistically associated?), predictive validity (does theory or previous research suggest other key variables which are expected to be predicted by our measure?) or criterion validity where we have a clearly agreed and defined measure which can be used to 'bench mark' our measure (see also *Reliability*).

Variables: These are the coded (numeric) out-turns of a survey questionnaire. Each individual or case is represented by a set of numbers which summarise each individual response (or absence of one) to a question. Individual codes or codes derived from more than one question have meaning only when the researcher brings information to each number (e.g. numbers as labels, numbers as strength of attachment, numbers as quantities). Unsurprisingly, the values of these numbers will vary across a sample, hence the generic term *variable*.

Check out the next title in the collection: Exploratory and Descriptive Statistics, for guidance on Exploratory and Descriptive Statistics.

REFERENCES

Adair, J. G. (1984). The Hawthorne effect: A reconsideration of the methodological artifact. *Journal of Applied Psychology, 69*(2), 334–345. https://doi.org/10.1037/0021-9010.69.2.334

Ahmad, W. (1999). 'Ethnic statistics: better than nothing or worse than nothing?' In Dorling, D. and Simpson, S. (Eds.) *Statistics and society: The arithmetic of politics* (pp. 124–131). Arnold.

Bauman, Z. (1999). *Liquid modernity*. Polity Press.

Bawin-Legros, B. (2004). Intimacy and the new sentimental order. *Current Sociology, 52*(2), 241–250. https://doi.org/10.1177/0011392104041810

Bellhouse, D. R. (1988). A brief history of random sampling methods. In P. R. Krishnaiah & C. R. Rao (Eds.), *Handbook of statistics* (Vol. 6, pp. 1–14). Elsevier Science. https://doi.org/10.1016/S0169-7161(88)06003-1

Bernard, J., Daňková, H., & Vašát, P. (2018). Ties, sites and irregularities: Pitfalls and benefits in using respondent-driven sampling for surveying a homeless population. *International Journal of Social Research Methodology, 21*(5), 603–618. https://doi.org/10.1080/13645579.2018.1454640

Blaikie, N. (2007). *Approaches to social enquiry* (2nd ed.). Cambridge University Press.

Blalock, H. (1961). *Causal inference in nonexperimental research*. University of North Carolina Press.

Blanchard, R. D., Bunker, J. B., & Wachs, M. (1977). Distinguishing aging, period and cohort effects in longitudinal studies of elderly populations. *Socio-Economic Planning Sciences, 11*(3), 137–146. https://doi.org/10.1016/0038-0121(77)90032-5

Blau, P., & Duncan, O. (1978). *The American occupational structure*. Free Press.

Bohannon, J. (2013). Who's afraid of peer review? *Science, 342*(6154), 60–65. https://doi.org/10.1126/science.342.6154.60

Bowling, A. (2005). Mode of questionnaire administration can have serious effects on data quality. *Journal of Public Health, 27*(3), 281–291. https://doi.org/10.1093/pubmed/fdi031

Bramley, G., & Fitzpatrick, S. (2018). Homelessness in the UK: Who is most at risk? *Housing Studies*, *33*(1), 96–116. https://doi.org/10.1080/02673037.2017.1344957

Buck, M., Bryant, L., & Williams, M. (1993). *Housing and households in Cornwall: A pilot study of Cornish families*. Department of Applied Social Science, University of Plymouth.

Bulmer, M. (2015). *The uses of social research (Routledge Revivals): Social investigation in public policy making*. Routledge. https://doi.org/10.4324/9781315697451

Byrne, D. (2002). *Interpreting quantitative data*. Sage. https://doi.org/10.4135/9781849209311

Byrne, D., & Ragin, C. (2009). *The SAGE handbook of case based methods*. Sage. https://doi.org/10.4135/9781446249413

Calderwood, L., & Lessof, C. (2009). Enhancing longitudinal surveys by linking to administrative data. In R. M. Groves, G. Kalton, J. N. K. Rao, N. Schwarz, C. Skinner, & P. Lynn (Eds.), *Methodology of longitudinal surveys* (pp. 55–72). Wiley. https://doi.org/10.1002/9780470743874.ch4

Callegaro, M., Manfreda, K. L., & Vehovar, V. (2015). *Web survey methodology*. Sage.

Cambridge University Press. (1995). Sampling. In *Cambridge International Dictionary of English*. Retrieved December 10, 2017, from https://dictionary.cambridge.org/dictionary/english/sampling

Campbell, D. T., & Stanley, J. C. (1963). Experimental and quasi-experimental designs on teaching. In N. L. Gage (Ed.), *Handbook of research on teaching* (pp. 171–246). Rand McNally.

Cannell, C. F., & Fowler, F. J. (1963). A comparison of self-enumerative procedure and a personal interview: A validity study. *Public Opinion Quarterly*, *27*(2), 250–264. https://doi.org/10.1086/267165

Cartwright, N. (2003). *Hunting causes and using them: Approaches in philosophy and economics*. Cambridge University Press.

Cartwright, N. (2004). Causation: One word, many things. *Philosophy of Science*, *71*(5), 805–819. https://doi.org/10.1086/426771

Champion, A. G. (1994). Population change in Britain since 1981: Evidence for continuing deconcentration. *Environment and Planning A: Economy and Space*, *26*(10), 1501–1520. https://doi.org/10.1068/a261501

Champion, T. (2001). Urbanisation, surburbanisation, counterurbanisation and reurbanisation. In R. Paddison (Ed.), *Handbook of urban studies* (pp. 143–161). Sage. https://doi.org/10.4135/9781848608375.n9

Collett, T., Williams, M., Maconachie, M., Chandler, J., & Dodgeon, B. (2006). 'Long termness' with regards to sickness and disability: An example of the value of longitudinal data for testing reliability and validity. *International Journal of Social Research Methodology*, *9*(3), 224–243. https://doi.org/10.1080/13645570600656462

Couper, M. P. (2008). *Designing effective web surveys.* Cambridge University Press. https://doi.org/10.1017/CBO9780511499371

Czaja, R., & Blair, J. (2005). *Designing surveys: A guide to decisions and procedures* (2nd ed.). Sage. https://doi.org/10.4135/9781412983877

Dale, A., & Marsh, C. (Eds.). (1993). *The 1991 census user's guide.* Her Majesty's Stationery Office.

de Vaus, D. A. (2001). *Research design in social research.* Sage.

de Vaus, D. A. (2014). *Surveys in social research* (6th ed.). Routledge. https://doi.org/10.4324/9780203519196

Devine, F., & Heath, S. (1999). *Sociological research methods in context.* Macmillan. https://doi.org/10.1007/978-1-349-27550-2

Dodgeon, B., Patalay, P., Ploubidis, G. B., & Wiggins, R. D. (2020). Exploring the role of early life circumstances, abilities and achievements on well-being at age 50 years: Evidence from the 1958 British Birth Cohort Study. *BMJ Open, 10*(2), Article e031416. https://doi.org/10.1136/bmjopen-2019-031416

Dorling, D. (2007). How many of us are there and where are we? Validation of the 2001 Census and its revisions. *Environment and Planning A: Economy and Space, 39*(5), 1024–1044. https://doi.org/10.1068/a38140

Drew, D., Fosam, B., & Gilborn, D. (1995). Race, IQ and the underclass: Don't believe the hype. *Radical Statistics,* (60), 2–21. www.radstats.org.uk/no060/drewetal.pdf

Durrant, G. B. (2005). *Imputation methods for handling non-response in the social sciences: A methodological review* (NCRM Methods Review Paper No. NCRM/002). ESRC National Centre for Research Methods. http://eprints.ncrm.ac.uk/86/1/MethodsReviewPaperNCRM-002.pdf

Elo, S., Kääriäinen, M., Isola, A., & Kyngäs, H. (2013). Developing and testing a middle-range theory of the well-being supportive physical environment of home-dwelling elderly. *Scientific World Journal, 2013,* Article 945635. https://doi.org/10.1155/2013/945635

Erens, B., Phelps, A., Clifton, S., Mercer, C. H., Tanton, C., Hussey, D., Sonnenberg, P., Macdowall, W., Field, N., Datta, J., Mitchell, K., Copas, A. J., Wellings, K., & Johnson, A. M. (2014). Methodology of the third British National Survey of Sexual Attitudes and Lifestyles (Natsal-3). *Sexually Transmitted Infections, 90*(2), 84–89. https://doi.org/10.1136/sextrans-2013-051359

Erikson, R., & Goldthorpe, J. (2010). Has social mobility in Britain decreased? Reconciling divergent findings on income and class mobility. *British Journal of Sociology, 61*(2), 211–230. https://doi.org/10.1111/j.1468-4446.2010.01310.x

Fecher, B., & Friesike, S. (2014). Open science: One term, five schools of thought. In S. Bartling & S. Friesike (Eds.), *Opening science: The evolving guide on how the internet is changing research, collaboration and scholarly publishing* (pp. 17–47). Springer. https://doi.org/10.1007/978-3-319-00026-8_2

Feller, W. (2008). *An introduction to probability: Theory and its applications* (2nd ed., Vol. 2). Wiley.

Ferri, C. P., Prince, M., Brayne, C., Brodaty, H., & Fratiglioni, L. (2005). Global prevalence of dementia: A Delphi consensus study. *Lancet, 266*(9503), 2112–2117. https://doi.org/10.1016/S0140-6736(05)67889-0

Field, A. (2018). *Discovering statistics using IBM SPSS statistics*. Sage.

Flick, U. (2016). *An introduction to qualitative research* (6th ed.). Sage.

Foster, K. (1993). The electoral register as a sampling frame. *Survey Methods Bulletin, 33*(7), 1–7.

Freedman, D. (2011). Statistical models and shoe leather. In A. Vayda & B. Walters (Eds.), *Causal explanation for social scientists* (pp. 151–167). Rowman & Littlefield.

Fugard, A. (2020). Should trans people be postmodernist in the streets but positivist in the spreadsheets? *International Journal of Social Research Methodology, 23*(5), 525–531. https://doi.org/10.1080/13645579.2020.1768343

Geoff, P., Judy, P., & Hyde, M. (1996). 'Refuse of all classes?' Social indicators and social deprivation. *Sociological Research Online, 1*(1), 50–68. https://doi.org/10.5153/sro.1293

Giddens, A. (1993). *New rules of sociological method: A positive critique of interpretative sociologies*. Stanford University Press.

Gillies, D. (2000). *Philosophical theories of probability*. Routledge.

Godfroy Genin, A.-S., & Pinault, C. (2011). The benefits of comparing grapefruits and tangerines: A toolbox for European cross-cultural comparisons in engineering education – Using this toolbox to study gendered images of engineering among students. *European Journal of Engineering Education, 31*(1), 22–33. https://doi.org/10.1080/03043790500429989

Goldthorpe, J. (1985). On economic development and social mobility. *British Journal of Sociology, 36*(4), 549–573. https://doi.org/10.2307/590331

Goldthorpe, J. (2016). Social class mobility in modern Britain: Changing structure, constant process. *Journal of the British Academy, 4*, 89–111. https://doi.org/10.5871/jba/004.089

Gough, D., Oliver, S., & Thomas, J. (2012). *An introduction to systematic reviews* (2nd ed.). Sage.

Gouldner, A. (1973). *For sociology: Renewal and critique in sociology today*. Penguin.

Greenaway, M., & Russ, B. (2016). *A guide to calculating standard errors for ONS social surveys* (ONS Methodology Working Paper Series No. 9). Office for National Statistics. www.ons.gov.uk/methodology/methodologicalpublications/generalmethodology/onsworkingpaperseries/onsmethodologyworkingpaperseriesno9guidetocalculatingstandarderrorsforonssocialsurveys#toc

Griffith, L., van den Heuvel, E., Fortier, I., Hofer, S., Raina, P., Sohel, N., Papette, H., Wolfson, C., & Belleville, S. (2013). *Harmonization of cognitive measures in individual participant data and aggregate data meta analysis* (Report No. 13-EHC040). Agency for Healthcare Research and Quality.

Groves, R. M. (2006). Nonresponse rates and nonresponse bias in household surveys. *Public Opinion Quarterly, 70*(5), 646–675. https://doi.org/10.1093/poq/nfl033

Groves, R. M. (2011). Three eras of survey research. *Public Opinion Quarterly, 76*(5), 861–871. https://doi.org/10.1093/poq/nfr057

Groves, R. M., Fowler, F. J., Jr., Couper, M. P., Lepkowski, J. M., Singer, E., & Tourangeau, R. (2009). *Survey methodology* (2nd ed.). Wiley.

Haig, J. (2012). Historical sketch. In *Probability: A very short introduction* (pp. 27–42). Oxford University Press. https://doi.org/10.1093/actr ade/9780199588480.003.0003

Haug, C. (2015). Peer-review fraud: Hacking the scientific publication process. *New England Journal of Medicine, 373*(25), 2393–2395. https://doi.org/10.1056/NEJMp1512330

Heckathorn, D. D. (1997). Respondent driven sampling: A new approach to the study of hidden populations. *Social Problems, 44*(2), 174–199. https://doi.org/10.2307/3096941

Higgins, J. P. T., Thomas, J., Chandaler, J., Cumpston, M., Li, T., Page, M. J., & Welch, V. A. (Eds.). (2019). *The Cochrane handbook for the systematic review of interventions* (2nd ed.). Wiley-Blackwell. https://doi.org/10.1002/9781119536604

Hobbs, G., & Vignoles, A. (2010). Is children's free school meal 'eligibility' a good proxy for family income? *British Educational Research Journal, 36*(4), 673–690. https://doi.org/10.1080/01411920903083111

Horowitz, I. (1967). *The rise and fall of Project Camelot*. MIT Press.

Jacobs, K., Kemeny, K., & Manzi, T. (2003). Privileged or exploited council tenants: The discursive change in conservative housing policy from 1972–1980. *Policy & Politics, 31*(3), 307–320. https://doi.org/10.1332/030557303322034965

Janack, M. (2002). Dilemmas of objectivity. *Social Epistemology, 16*(3), 267–281. https://doi.org/10.1080/0269172022000025624

Joshi, H., & Fitzsimmons, E. (2016). The Millennium Cohort Study: The making of a multi-purpose resource for social science and policy. *Longitudinal and Life Course Studies, 7*(4), 409–430. https://doi.org/10.14301/llcs.v7i4.410

Jowell, R. (1986). The codification of statistical ethics. *Journal of Official Statistics, 2*(3), 217–253.

Jowell, R., Roberts, C., Fitizgerald, R., Eva, G. (Eds.) (2007). *Measuring attitudes cross nationally: Lessons from the European Social Survey*. Sage.

Kalton, G., & Flores-Cervantes, I. (2003). Weighting methods. *Journal of Official Statistics*, *19*(2), 81–97.

Kincaid, H. (1996). *Philosophical foundations of the social sciences: Analyzing controversies in social research*. Cambridge University Press. https://doi.org/10.1017/CBO9780511625442

Kish, L. (1965). *Survey sampling*. Wiley.

Krosnick, J. A., Narajam, S., & Smith, W. R. (1996). *Satisficing in surveys: Initial evidence*. Wiley. https://doi.org/10.1002/ev.1033

Laslett, P. (1989). *A fresh map of life: The emergence of the third age*. Weidenfeld & Nicolson.

Lavrakas, P. J. (2008). *Encyclopaedia of survey research methods*. Sage. https://doi.org/10.4135/9781412963947

Layard, R. (2006). Happiness and public policy: A challenge to the profession. *Economic Journal*, *116*(150), C24–C33. https://doi.org/10.1111/j.1468-0297.2006.01073.x

Linacre, J. (2002). Optimizing rating scale category effectiveness. *Journal of Applied Measurement*, *3*(1), 85–106.

Litwin, M. (1995). *How to measure survey reliability and validity*. Sage. https://doi.org/10.4135/9781483348957

Litwin, M. (2003). *How to assess and interpret survey psychometrics* (2nd ed.). Sage. https://doi.org/10.4135/9781412984409

Longino, H. (1990). *Science as social knowledge: Values and objectivity in scientific enquiry*. Princeton University Press. https://doi.org/10.1515/9780691209753

Marsh, C. (1982). *The survey method: The contribution of surveys to sociological explanation*. Allen & Unwin.

Marsh, C., & Scarborough, E. (1990). Testing nine hypotheses about quota sampling. *Journal of the Market Research Society*, *32*(4), 485–506.

Merton, R. (1968). *Social theory and social structure*. Free Press.

Meyer, B. D., & Mittag, N. (2019). *Combining administrative and survey data to improve income measurement* (Working Paper No. 25738). National Bureau of Economic Research. https://doi.org/10.3386/w25738

Mostafa, T., & Wiggins, R. D. (2015). The impact of attrition and non-response in birth cohort studies: A need to incorporate missingness strategies. *Longitudinal and Life Course Studies*, *6*(2), 131–146. https://doi.org/10.14301/llcs.v6i2.312

Musgrove, F. (1963). *The migratory elite*. Heinemann.

Newcomb, M. D., & Bentler, P. M. (1988). Impact of adolescent drug use and social support on problems of young adults: A longitudinal study. *Journal of Abnormal Psychology*, *97*(1), 64–75. https://doi.org/10.1037/0021-843X.97.1.64

Newton-Smith, W. (1981). *The rationality of science*. Routledge & Kegan Paul.

Nolan, D. (1997). Quantitative parsimony. *British Journal for Philosophy of Science*, *48*(3), 329–343. https://doi.org/10.1093/bjps/48.3.329

Oakes, J. M., & Johnson, J. P. (2006). Propensity score matching for social epidemiology. In J. M. Oakes & J. S. Kaufman (Eds.), *Methods in social epidemiology* (1st ed., pp. 370–393). Wiley.

Office for National Statistics. (2017). *User guide to crime statistics for England & Wales*. www.ons.gov.uk

Oppenheim, A. (1992). *Questionnaire design, interviewing and attitude measurement*. Pinter.

Pallant, J. (2020). *SPSS survival guide to data analysis using IBM SPSS* (7th ed.). Blackwell.

Pawson, R. (2000). Middle-range realism. *European Journal of Sociology/ Archive Européenes de Sociologie*, *41*(2), 283–325. https://doi.org/10.1017/ S0003975600007050

Popper, K. (1966). *The open society and its enemies: Vol. 2. The high tide of prophecy: Hegel, Marx and the aftermath*. Routledge & Kegan Paul.

Popper, K. (1968). *Conjectures and refutations: The growth of scientific knowledge*. Harper & Row.

Proctor, R. (1991). *Value free science: Purity and power in modern knowledge*. Harvard University Press.

Riegg, S. K. (2008). Causal inference and omitted variable bias in financial aid research: Assessing solutions. *Review of Higher Education*, *31*(3), 329–354. https:// doi.org/10.1353/rhe.2008.0010

Rosenbaum, P. R., & Rubin, D. (1983). The central role of the propensity score in observational studies of causal effects. *Biometrika*, *70*(1), 41–55. https://doi. org/10.1093/biomet/70.1.41

Rowland, D. T. (2012). The Third Age. In D. T. Rowland (Ed.), *Population aging: The transformation of societies* (pp. 167–181). Springer. https://doi.org/10.1007/978-94-007-4050-1_11

Rubin, D. (2008). Statistical inference for causal effects, with emphasis on applications in epidemiology and medical statistics. In C. Rao, J. Miller, & D. Rao (Eds.), *Handbook of statistics, epidemiology and medical statistics* (Vol. *27*, pp. 28–63). Elsevier. https://doi.org/10.1016/S0169-7161(07)27002-6

Rutter, M., Tizard, J., & Whitmore, K. (1970). *Education, health and behaviour*. Longman.

Saunders, P. (1990). *A nation of home owners*. Unwin Hyman.

Savage, M., & Burrows, R. (2007). The coming crisis of empirical sociology. *Sociology*, *41*(5), 885–899. https://doi.org/10.1177/0038038507080443

Schlipp, P. (Ed.). (1991). *The philosophy of Rudolph Carnap*. Open Court.

Setia, M. S. (2016). Methodological series module 1: Cohort studies. *Indian Journal of Dermatology*, *61*(1), 21–25. https://doi.org/10.4103/0019-5154.174011

Sloan, L. (2017). Who tweets in the United Kingdom? Profiling the Twitter population using the British Social Attitudes Survey 2015. *Social Media + Society*, *3*(1). https://doi.org/10.1177/2056305117698981

Stahl, S. A., & Miller, P. D. (1989). A whole language and language experience for beginning reading: A quantitative research synthesis. *Review of Education Research*, *59*(1), 87–116. https://doi.org/10.3102/00346543059001087

Stephens, C., & Sukumar, R. (2006). Introduction to data mining, In R. Grover & M. Vriens (Eds.), *The handbook of marketing research* (pp/ 455–485). Sage.

Stinchcombe, A. L. (1968). *Constructing social theories*. Chicago University Press.

Stouffer, S. (1949). *The American soldier*. Princeton University Press.

Stuart, A. (1964). *Basic ideas of scientific sampling* (2nd ed.). Charles Griffin.

Sudman, S. (1966). Probability sampling with quotas. *Journal of the American Statistical Association*, *61*(315), 749–771. https://doi.org/10.1080/01621459.1966.10480903

Sudman, S., & Cowan, C. D. (1988). Sampling rare and elusive populations. *Science*, *240*(4855), 991–996. https://doi.org/10.1126/science.240.4855.991

Sullivan, A. (2020). Sex and the census: Why surveys should not conflate sex and gender identity. *International Journal of Social Research Methodology*, *23*(5), 517–524. https://doi.org/10.1080/13645579.2020.1768346

Sykes, W., & Collins, M. (1992). Anatomy of the survey interview. *Journal of Official Statistics*, *8*(3), 277–291.

Tarnopolsky, A., Barker, S. M., Wiggins, R. D., & McLean, E. K. (1978). The effect of aircraft noise on the mental health of a community sample: A pilot study. *Psychological Medicine*, *8*(2), 219–233. https://doi.org/10.1017/S0033291700014276

Tarnopolsky, A., Hand, D. J., McLean, E. K., Roberts, H., & Wiggins, R. D. (1979). Validity and uses of a screening questionnaire in the community. *British Journal of Psychiatry*, *134*(5), 508–519. https://doi.org/10.1192/bjp.134.5.508

Tarnopolsky, A., & Morton-Williams, J. (1980). *Aircraft noise and psychiatric morbidity: Research report*. Social and Community Planning Research.

Tashakkori, A., & Teddle, C. (2010). *The SAGE handbook of mixed methods for the social and behavioural sciences* (2nd ed.). Sage. https://doi.org/10.4135/9781506335193

Tennant, R., Hiller, L., Fishwick, R., Platt, S., Joseph, S., Weich, S., Parkinson, J., Secker, J., & Stewart-Brown, S. (2007). The Warwick–Edinburgh mental well-being scale (WEMWBS): Development and UK validation. *Health and Quality of Life Outcomes*, *5*, Article 63. https://doi.org/10.1186/1477-7525-5-63

Thomas, R., & Purdon, S. (1994). Telephone methods for social surveys. *Social Research Update*, (8), 1–6. https://sru.soc.surrey.ac.uk/SRU8.html

Tourangeau, R., Conrad, F., & Couper, M. (2013). *The science of web surveys*. Oxford University Press. https://doi.org/10.1093/acprof:oso/9780199747047.001.0001

Vogt, W. P. (2007). *Quantitative research methods for professionals*. Pearson.

Ware, L., Maconachie, M., Williams, M., Chandler, J., & Dodgeon, B. (2007). Gender life course transitions from the nuclear family in England and Wales 1981–2001. *Sociological Research Online*, *12*(4), 49–60. https://doi.org/10.5153/sro.1544

Weber, M. (1949). *The methodology of the social sciences*. Free Press.

Wickham, H., & Grolemund, G. (2017). *R for data science: Import, tidy, transform, visualize and model data*. Blackwell.

Wiggins, R. D., Netuveli, G., Hyde, M., Higgs, P., & Blane, D. (2008). The evaluation of a self-enumerated scale of quality of life (CASP-19) in the context of research on ageing: A combination of exploratory and confirmatory approaches. *Social Indicators Research*, *89*(1), 61–77. https://doi.org/10.1007/s11205-007-9220-5

Williams, M. (2000). Interpretivism and generalisation. *Sociology*, *34*(2), 209–224. https://doi.org/10.1017/S0038038500000146

Williams, M. (2003). The problem of representation: Realism and operationalism in survey research. *Sociological Research Online*, *8*(1), 81–91. https://doi.org/10.5153/sro.779

Williams, M. (2006). Can scientists be objective? *Social Epistemology*, *20*(2), 163–180. https://doi.org/10.1080/02691720600807468

Williams, M. (2016). *Key concepts in the philosophy of social research*. Sage. https://doi.org/10.4135/9781473982758

Williams, M. (2018). Making up mechanisms in realist research. In N. Emmel, J. Greenhalgh, A. Manzano, M. Monaghan, & S. Dalkin (Eds.), *Doing realist research* (pp. 25–40). Sage. https://doi.org/10.4135/9781526451729.n3

Williams, M. (2021). *Realism and complexity in social science*. Routledge.

Williams, M., & Champion, T. (1998). Cornwall, poverty and in migration. In P. Payton (Ed.), *Cornish studies* (2nd Series, Vol. 6, pp. 118–126). University of Exeter Press.

Williams, M., & Cheal, B. (2001). Is there any such thing as homelessness? Measurement, explanation and process in 'homelessness' research. *Innovation: European Journal of Social Research*, *14*(3), 239–253. https://doi.org/10.1080/13511610120102600

Williams, M., & Dale, A. (1991). *Measuring housing deprivation using the OPCS Longitudinal Study* (LS Working Paper No. 72). SSRU.

Williams, M., & Husk, K. (2013). Can we, should we measure ethnicity? *International Journal of Social Research Methodology*, *16*(4), 285–300. https://doi.org/10.1080/13645579.2012.682794

Williams, M., Payne, G., & Hodgkinson, L. (2008). Does sociology count? Student attitudes to the teaching of quantitative methods. *Sociology*, *42*(5), 1003–1022. https://doi.org/10.1177/0038038508094576

Williams, M., Sloan, L., & Brookfield, C. (2017). A tale of two sociologies: Analysis versus critique in UK sociology. *Sociological Research Online*, *22*(4), 132–151. https://doi.org/10.1177/1360780417734146

Williams, M. L., Burnap, P., & Sloan, L. (2016). Crime sensing with big data: The affordances and limitations of using open source communications to estimate crime patterns. *British Journal of Criminology*, *57*(2), 320–334. https://doi.org/10.1093/bjc/azw031

Wilson, W. (1997). *When work disappears: The world of the new urban poor*. Vintage.

Zmerli, S., & Hooghe, M. (Eds.). (2011). *Political trust: Why context matters*. ECPR Press.

INDEX

Printed in Great Britain
by Amazon

78133741R00115